FIRE ON THE MOUNTAIN

Norma R. Youngberg

Pacific Press®
Publishing Association

Nampa, Idaho | Oshawa, Ontario, Canada
www.pacificpress.com

Cover art by John Steel
Inside design by Pacific Press® Publishing Association

Copyright © 2014 edition by Pacific Press® Publishing Association
Printed in the United States of America
All rights reserved

The author assumes full responsibility for the accuracy of all facts and quotations as cited in this book.

You can obtain additional copies of this book by calling toll-free 1-800-765-6955 or by visiting www.adventistbookcenter.com. You can purchase this as an e-book by visiting www.adventist-ebooks.com.

ISBN 13: 978-0-8163-1962-6
ISBN 10: 0-8163-1962-6

November 2014

Contents

1. The Escape 5
2. The Feast 14
3. Visitors 21
4. Preparing a Curse 30
5. Singing Water 37
6. The Trusting Heart 44
7. A Message for Uncle Sobat 51
8. Call Rajin 58
9. The Angel 66
10. Flame of Fury 74
11. The Mustard Seed 82
12. Vee-Vee 89

CHAPTER 1

The Escape

AMONG the hills of Borneo there is a sparkling pool set like a jewel in a hollow of the rocks—a pool so clear that it looks as though a child might wade through it; but it is fully twenty feet deep. There it lies, surrounded by grassy slopes and a great forest of trees. The stream that feeds it flows down the mountain over a stony bed, steep and long, and the sound of its rapids can be heard for a long distance.

There is a Dusun village clinging to the green slope above the pool, and the music of the river has given the village its name—Singing Water.

It was in this village of Singing Water that something wonderful happened. The time was not long ago. The season was summer. It is always summertime in those mountains.

Saksee stood on the edge of the shining pool early in the morning. He studied his reflection in the water. As he looked into the blue mirror he was pleased with what he saw. No twelve-year-old boy in the mountains was stronger or better formed than he. He mumbled a few words to himself.

"This is the last day! The last day!" he moved his lips but

made no sound. The truth was that Saksee hardly knew whether he was happy or sad. He would go home this afternoon to his own village of Broken Light. After living for five years in Singing Water he was going away—six miles up the mountain, back home to his father's house. He had lived in Singing Water ever since his mother died. He was only seven years old then. He had come to live with his father's brother, Uncle Sobat, and his wife, Aunt Gar.

Once he had loved this village, but now it had become unbearable. Once it was safe and beautiful. Now it was spoiled. He had talked the matter over with Kooning, the witch doctor in his own village. Kooning advised him to return to his father's house in Broken Light.

Saksee heard a sound. It came from behind a large rock at the water's edge. It was the sound of words. Some person was talking. He could not hear much of what was being said. He could catch only one word—*bapa,* which means "father." The word was repeated several times. There was only one voice, and no one answered it.

With quiet, catlike steps Saksee crept down closer, until he could see what was behind the rock. He stood very still and scarcely breathed. He saw just what he might have expected—that new teacher, Rajin. Rajin was there behind the rock, and he was alone; yet he was talking to someone. He was kneeling on the sand. His eyes were closed and his hands were lifted. His face was covered with gladness. Saksee marked how his black hair curled at the temples and over his high forehead. He could see the scar Rajin had on one cheek. He saw the strength in the young teacher's raised hands and arms. His white shirt was open at the throat and he wore dark cotton trousers like the ones Saksee had on.

The boy turned away, slipped off his clothes, and slid into the water without a sound. Like all the boys of this village, he was an excellent swimmer. He moved through the clear water like a brown fish. As he circled and swam he remembered that there was no pool of water like this in his own village of Broken Light. The people there drew their water from a spring trickling down the mountainside. He would miss his daily dips in the pool. He would miss Uncle Sobat and Aunt Gar and little Vee-Vee, their small daughter.

Well, it couldn't be helped. Ever since the new teaching had come to Singing Water he had felt troubled and uneasy—uncomfortable. Kooning's advice was good. He would go back to Broken Light, where the old witch doctor ordered everything according to the customs their tribe had observed for hundreds of years. No one in Broken Light planted or harvested or married without advice from Kooning. They were fortunate to have him live among them. Even the people in Singing Water called on him for charms and advice, because they had no regular witch doctor of their own.

Now this new teacher had come. Kooning told all the people in both villages to pay no attention to the stranger.

"This teaching is bad. Listening to it is like drinking poisonous liquor," he said. "It makes people happy, but it destroys all the old customs and makes the spirits angry. The end will be trouble. You boys stay away from it."

Then the old man had turned to Saksee. His long yellow teeth clicked together as he talked. "You must return to your father's house in our own village. You are big enough to help him now. You don't need your aunt's care any more. You can cut the brush and carry the wood and boil the rice."

Saksee steadied himself in the pool. He was thinking about

how it all had happened. Rajin's voice startled him.

"Peaceful morning to you!" the teacher called.

"Peaceful morning to you!" Saksee answered, according to the polite custom of his people.

"You swim well." Rajin watched the lad skim and dive for several minutes. "Perhaps I shall do better when I have been here as long as you have."

Saksee didn't answer these words. But he thought in his heart, This man plans to stay here a long time—a long time. The poison of his teaching will spread everywhere and all will be spoiled. I'm glad I'm going back to Broken Light.

The boy crawled out of the water and snatched up his scanty garments from the grassy slope.

Then Rajin called to him. "Come sing with us tonight. It is a great pleasure to sing, don't you think so?"

Saksee turned to look at the teacher, who now was swimming in the pool. His body was as brown and lithe as his own, and his features were similar to those of the people in Singing Water Village; yet he was different. There was a sharp cleanness about him and a radiance of happiness that made him always gay. His voice had the sound of joy and laughter in it. Saksee felt angry.

"I shall not come to sing," he said in a low voice. "Today I will go back to my own village."

Hearing this, the teacher, Rajin, leaped out of the pool and stood beside him. "Are you going to the village of Broken Light? Are you going to stay there?"

"Yes, I will stay there always," the boy replied.

Rajin laid a hand on the boy's shoulder. "You have heard some of the teaching about God. You know that He is our great Father up in heaven." He pointed to the sky. "You know

The Escape 9

that He can always help you in any trouble. Even in your village He is close to you. Talk to Him. He will hear you."

Saksee drew away from the friendly grasp of the teacher, and without more words he scrambled up the hill and hurried to his uncle's house.

When Saksee had come to live with Uncle Sobat and Aunt Gar, Vee-Vee was a baby not big enough to walk. Now she was six years old.

Saksee came into the kitchen room of the little hut. Aunt Gar smiled at him. "Come now, eat your rice." She ladled out a portion of hot rice onto a banana leaf. She put some boiled vegetables and a few small dried fish with it. He sat down on the floor and began eating with his fingers. The breakfast tasted good. He remembered all the good meals Aunt Gar had cooked for him. Now when he got home to Broken Light he would have to cook his own rice. There was no woman in his father's house. Saksee was big enough to do the cooking for them both. Kooning, the witch doctor, had said so.

Vee-Vee sat on the floor beside him, eating her own rice. She was big for her age, but she sat quietly and said nothing. In all her life she had never spoken a single word. She could cry and make queer noises of pain or surprise, but she could neither hear nor speak. Perhaps for this reason Uncle Sobat loved the child with more than ordinary tenderness. Even Saksee felt a fierce affection for the little girl whose face and body were so perfect, yet who had no hearing and no words.

While Saksee ate his food the little child looked toward him often, and smiled in a questioning way. She seemed to feel some uneasiness in his manner. Could she guess that he was leaving today?

By midday he was ready to go. All he owned was in the

bohongan on his back. He had few belongings, so Aunt Gar had filled the bark container with fat sections of sugar cane and some fruit from the trees along the river. The *bohongan* was heavily loaded, and the boy bent his naked back under it as he climbed the steep trail toward the village of Broken Light.

Saksee was glad the teacher had not seen him leave. Rajin would have talked to him some more about God. He wanted none of that. He was leaving this place and this hateful teaching. He would not need to worry about it any more. He regretted now that he had stayed so long. It must be two moons since Rajin came to Singing Water.

Every night Rajin gathered the people and taught them songs about the God of heaven. He taught them from the Book of his magic. Saksee had gone to listen. He could recall many of the words from the Book. He remembered more of the songs because the melody and the rhyming of the words made them slip easily into the mind and fasten themselves there.

Never mind! He would soon forget. He would follow the good advice of Kooning, the witchman, and all must turn out well. He might even become a witch doctor himself one of these days when he became old enough.

He was out of sight of the village now. There could be no harm in resting. He loosened the straps of the *bohongan* from his forehead and his arms. He set the heavy bark carrier down beside the path and perched on a damp root while the breeze cooled his head and dried the sweat that streamed down his lean body.

His attention was attracted by a swarm of caterpillars clustered on the trunk of a tree across the path. Saksee knew they were poison. He would not touch one for anything. They burned like fire; but it was interesting to watch them. They moved like an army up the trunk of the tree. They crowded so close together that their gray-green bodies covered the bark for a couple feet. One could not see the bark at all, they were so close and thick. Saksee knew that if a man chanced to brush against a tree infested with poison caterpillars there would be terrible consequences. His uncle had often warned him. Still for a long time he sat fascinated by this evil thing so close to him.

"It's just like the teaching of Rajin," the boy said out loud. "It is running all over Singing Water Village; but it can't hurt me if I don't touch it."

He got to his feet and fastened the heavy *bohongan* to his back. Again he began to climb the steep side of the mountain. He stopped to rest often, and whenever he sat down and rested he thought about Rajin and the new teaching. He became angry with himself.

"Can't I get that fellow out of my mind?" he sputtered to himself.

He tried to think of his home in Broken Light. He had visited there often since his mother's death. He knew exactly how it would be. His father, Pakoo, was an important man in the village. He owned several water buffaloes. He raised a fine garden every year and a field of mountain rice. He saved plenty of the rice for wine, and one of the chief pleasures in Broken Light Village was drinking rice wine.

The boy's heart skipped with pleasure as he thought of the long evenings when the rice wine would be passed around and the tom-toms would throb out their weird sweet music while the dancers swayed and reeled to the beat of the drums on the village green.

It used to be that way in Singing Water; but since Rajin came, there was no more time for the drums and drunken dancing. Almost everyone wanted to go up to the teacher's house and listen to the stories he told, and to join in the songs.

Then Saksee thought of the clear pool below Singing Water. With sharp clearness the scene of this morning came back to him. He saw again the face of the teacher raised to the heavens and heard the word *bapa*. He remembered the look on Rajin's face. He shook himself in torment. "I do believe that teacher has bewitched me with his magic!" Once again he resolved to think no more about the matter.

With a start he saw that the sun was going down—and he was not yet home. He tried to hurry; but he had already dallied too much along the way. Now it was impossible to reach his house before dark. Fear took hold of him. He tugged at the heavy *bohongan*. He even thought of leaving it there in the path and running home as fast as he could. But to do such a thing would brand him a coward.

His breath came in painful heaves. His shoulders ached and his head throbbed. He stumbled up the mountain in the failing light. Now he was barely able to see the way.

This would never do! He slowed down and climbed carefully. Now he was very quiet. The creatures of the night had come out in the forest. He knew what they were—the leopard cats, the fierce Malayan bears, and the huge wild cattle called *timbado*, who would stalk a man on the trail and gore him to death with their horns. Then there were the wild pigs—great evil creatures with razor-sharp tusks. One blow from such a tusk could kill a man if it struck him in the stomach or chest. Then there were the night-crawling snakes. Saksee shuddered. He felt paralyzed!

Then he heard a slight sound—something was creeping along the path. Or was it in the brush? What could it be? The frightened boy drew his belt knife and leaned his *bohongan* against a tree. He stood with it still fastened to his back. It would protect him from one direction. He lifted his knife and peered into the darkness, waiting.

CHAPTER 2

The Feast

SAKSEE crouched in the path with his back against the *bohongan* and his belt knife raised to deal with any wild beast that might rush upon him. The sounds had stopped. The jungle was quiet, but his terror remained. His mouth felt dry and bitter. His hands shook and the strength of his body seemed to melt away.

Then words came to him—not words that could be heard with the ear, but words that hung close in the air and compelled his heart to listen. They were the words Rajin had spoken that morning by the pool below Singing Water: "He can always help you in any kind of trouble. Talk to Him. He will hear you."

The boy felt a great sob pressing up in his throat. His mind rejected the thought of Rajin's God; but his heart in its terror was like a small, pitiful creature running to any refuge that opened before it. Without wanting to—without meaning to—his thoughts flew to the God of heaven.

A light flashed in the path that led to his village. That light and the crashing and grunting in the brush showed him that his companion in the darkness was a wild pig. Frightened by the light, the pig scrambled off into the jungle.

A voice called to him through the night. It was his father, Pakoo. He held a burning torch in his hand.

"Saksee, Saksee!" the light came closer, "are you there?" His father must have heard the noise of the wild pig. The boy was too surprised and relieved to answer at once. His father had almost reached the spot where he stood with his back against the tree when he spoke.

"I am here, Father." He felt weak all over, and the cold sweat stood out on his face and shoulders.

"Kooning said you would come today and I began to worry about you. I was afraid you might have been delayed and be in some danger. It is good you have come." Then his father lifted the heavy *bohongan,* unfastening it from Saksee's arms and head. He placed it on his own back and carried it to the house in Broken Light—the house where Saksee had been born.

Pakoo had prepared rice and now he set food before his son. "Eat, and then rest awhile before you go to bathe."

Saksee felt so tired that the food had little attraction for him. He only picked at it. His father sat beside him and asked him many questions about the new teaching that had come to Singing Water.

"Is it true that the medicine of Rajin cures sick people?"

"Maybe," the boy answered. "But people are also helped by Kooning's medicine."

"Tell me," the older man's eyes glistened in the light from the coconut-oil lamp, "tell me, how does your Uncle Sobat, my brother, feel about this new witchcraft?"

"Uncle Sobat and Aunt Gar go every night to hear the words and sing the songs. So does everyone else in the village." Saksee left off eating and sat looking at his father.

Pakoo was a thick-set man with powerful arms and legs. His face appeared heavy. Only his keen eyes gave life to it. He was known to be a quiet man who loved the jungle. He was a great hunter. Once he lost his way among the mountains and lived for several days on the shoots of the wild jungle fern called *pakoo*. Thus he got his name, and it had stuck to him through the years.

"You are tired from the hard climb up the mountain," Pakoo said to his son. "Go, bathe. Then you must sleep. There will be time to talk tomorrow."

Saksee took a clean pair of short dark trousers from the *bohongan* and went to the spring to bathe. The spring discharged a fine stream of water right in the middle of the village. The people had guided it down the mountain in a series of giant bamboo lengths laid on a rude trestle. They had placed flat stones where the bamboo spouted the clear water so the earth would not be washed away.

Saksee remembered the pool at Singing Water. Would he ever dip in that pool again? Would he always have to bathe like this, standing on a stone with a stream of water washing over him?

The boy felt better after his bath. He went to his sleeping mat. In spite of his weariness he found it hard to sleep. His mind went back to the terrible moment on the path. He recalled how, for just an instant, his heart had gone out to the God of heaven. He hadn't wanted to. He hated the God of heaven! Yet in his fright he had almost turned to Him—almost—perhaps in his heart he really had called on God, the God of Rajin! Then came the light in the path and his father's voice calling his name. Could the God of heaven answer so quickly? He felt prickly all over and his heart beat fast. He twisted and turned on his mat. When he did fall asleep he wakened often, and the tune of a song rippled through his mind—a song Rajin had taught the people of Singing Water.

When the morning sunshine streamed through the tiny window above his mat Saksee wakened and sat up. For a moment he couldn't think where he was. Then he remembered. He was home in his own village, safe in his father's house.

"Peaceful morning to you!" Kooning called in front of the door.

"Peaceful morning," Pakoo answered, opening the door wide.

"I have a good thought," the witch doctor said, coming in and settling himself on a mat. "Our son has come home to stay. Shouldn't we have a little celebration in honor of his return? You have some fine rice wine and I have some. We could make a little feast and have some dancing and music. Then the boy will feel and know that we are glad he is home to stay."

"That's a fine idea!" Saksee's father looked at him. "You would like that, wouldn't you?"

The boy nodded his head. "I have been looking forward to our drinking parties and dancing," he said. "There is nothing like that in the village of Singing Water any more."

Kooning shook his head in grave sadness. "That's too bad. That abominable teaching spoils everything!" He stamped his foot and shook his clenched fist. "We will keep all the old customs lively here in this village. Perhaps some of the people from Singing Water will move up here and get away from that God-teacher and his witchcraft."

Kooning was a small man, old and dried out like a green fruit that has lain for a long time in the sun. His hair was thin and a little gray. His nose stood up from his face more than is usual in the Dusun people, and it was sharper than ordinary. His yellow teeth were loose and they clattered when he talked fast or became excited. He was a restless fellow. His hands were always working, twisting together, waving about, or gesturing furiously while he talked.

Kooning talked a lot. He knew everyone's business and nothing went on in the village without his supervision. There was a peculiar glittering quality about his eyes. They were not bright or clear. Years of drinking had taken away any freshness of expression that might have been there; but there was something sharp and sly about them. Saksee looked straight into Kooning's eyes as he spoke.

"Do you think if you went to the village of Singing Water you could persuade Uncle Sobat and Aunt Gar to stop going to that teacher's house?"

"I have already talked to Sobat." The old man waved his hands and shook them back and forth in a gesture of hopelessness. "I talked to him and he answered me that he will hear all about this new teaching first; then he will decide."

At sundown two days later the drums were brought and placed on the grassy slope near the bathing place in the center of the village. The women and children squatted in a circle about the spot. Rice wine was passed around. The drinking began. Even the musicians stopped frequently to gulp from coconut shells full of liquor. Then the beating of the drums and tom-toms took on a fiercer, faster rhythm.

A young man swayed to the center of the circle and began a wild dance. As he wagged and twisted his almost-naked body he waved his hands in meaningful gestures and chanted an old tribal song.

Another man joined him, and the two entertained the

company for several minutes. Then two women took up the dance and the chant.

The moon came out full and round and looked down on the scene through the great jungle trees and the coconut palms. Saksee sat in the circle, watching. The moonlight seemed almost as bright as day. A woman brought him a big coconut cup brimming with rice wine. He sipped a little. For more than two months he had not tasted any wine. Even before that, Uncle Sobat had never let him have more than a sip or two. Uncle Sobat said it was not good for young people to drink wine.

Now the people were watching him. They knew this feast was in his honor. They expected him to enjoy himself. He lifted the cup and drained it, then sat back feeling that at last he was a man. Here he was in his own village, with a feast to honor him, and he could toss down a coconut shellful of wine as well as the best of them.

Then he began to have an uneasy feeling in his middle. His stomach rejected the sudden drenching with liquor. He got up and ran to the back of his father's house. He was violently sick! He lay on the ground, rolling about in distress until he felt better. Then he went back to his place among the watching people.

The sound of the drums and the tom-toms was terrific. His head felt ready to burst. Surely they could hear this noise all the way down the mountain. They could certainly hear it in Singing Water. It was only six miles away. Then he remembered—no, they could not hear. They were all gathered in Rajin's house singing. The sound of the singing would drown out all other noises.

The boy was startled by his own thoughts. Where was the gladness of this feast—the gladness he remembered? Where was the happiness of this group of villagers gathered under the stars and the coconut palms, drinking and making this frightful racket? This was not as he had expected—not like his memories. Something must be wrong!

As the night advanced, the drinking and dancing were made more hideous by the shouts of drunken people. Early in the morning the dancing stopped. Most of the men were drunk; among them the chief of Broken Light and his son, Jawab, a tall lad of sixteen years. They wobbled to their feet and began to argue in loud voices. It was impossible to understand what the quarrel was about. They began to scream at each other and strike out with their fists. Finally they locked together in a fierce struggle.

The young man, Jawab, was slender and quick. He was a fine-looking fellow. The whole village knew that he would be chief someday. The old chief was stocky and heavy, with great strength.

The two wrestlers dragged and pushed and clawed each other. They were coming closer to the spot where Saksee sat. He stood up and backed up a few steps. Then with a burst of fury the old chief threw his son to the ground in sudden victory. The young man went down with a terrible scream.

Kooning, the witch doctor, hurried to him. One leg stuck out from his side at a grotesque angle. It seemed to be unjointed at the hip. The young man was in frightful pain. He screamed in agony for several minutes in spite of his mother who tried to speak comforting words to him. Then he lapsed into unconsciousness. After all, he was very drunk. The old chief sank down exhausted on the ground. It was plain that he had no idea of what had happened. He too was filled with rice wine. He began to snore.

CHAPTER 3

Visitors

ON the trampled grass in the moonlight the chief lay beside his son, Jawab. The women gathered around and looked at Jawab's terribly injured leg. They began to wail and grieve. They all knew that Jawab was the only living child of his old parents—the youngest of seven children. The others had all died in babyhood. Now the chief's only son was gravely injured—and by his own father—in a drunken fight.

Kooning and Pakoo looked at each other. They had been drinking too, but not so much as the others. They realized that a dreadful thing had happened.

"Now, what shall we do?" Pakoo asked the witch doctor.

Kooning twisted his hands together in a frenzy of worry and fright. "He can never walk again!" the old witchman whispered. "It is the anger of the spirits. He can never be chief! Who ever saw a chief with his leg sticking out like that?"

The young man moved in his drunken stupor. His breath came in dry snores and he moaned with every movement of his chest. With Saksee's help they moved him to his father's house, which was only a short distance away and near the hut of Pakoo. There they laid him on a mat. Saksee was left alone with Jawab for a moment while the other two men went to drag in the old chief.

The boy stood looking down at Jawab. A strange thought crossed his mind. What about the God of Rajin? Could He help someone with a trouble like this? No one in the village of Broken Light knew what to do. God—God—the thought of God frightened him. Where had it come from? He felt sickness rising again in his stomach. It must be almost morning. The eastern mountain was showing a faint glow.

When Pakoo and Kooning had dragged the chief to his mat in the same room, they came to stare at Jawab. Then Kooning hurried out the door. He had gone to fetch his charms, of course.

"Father!" Saksee took hold of Pakoo's hand. It was cold and shaking.

"Father!" Then the words came, forced from his unwilling throat. "The teacher Rajin—at Singing Water—he might know what to do!"

Pakoo looked at Saksee. Then he turned to see if Kooning might be lingering at the door. The trembling man fixed his clouded eyes on the lad. "You have been home only three days and already you want to send for the God-teacher!" There was anger in his face.

"I don't want to! I don't want to," Saksee insisted, "but I feel sorry for Jawab! It's hurting him so much! How can his leg get better if it is not pulled back straight again?"

Pakoo did not answer. In a minute Kooning came into the room. In one hand he carried a dried crocodile. In the other a bag of charms. His face was dark with fury. "What's this you say?" he turned on Saksee, screaming his anger. "That leg will stay exactly as it is unless it goes back by itself. We will not have that teacher coming to this village and spoiling all our pleasures as he has done in Singing Water."

The chief's wife had called all her relatives. A crowd was beginning to gather. Saksee felt faint and ill. He slipped out the door and ran to his father's hut and threw himself on his sleeping mat. When he wakened it was broad daylight. The sun was halfway to the zenith and he heard voices outside—voices that he recognized.

He leaped from his mat and hurried out. Uncle Sobat and Rajin stood there in the hot sunshine. His father was talking with them. Saksee was too amazed to speak. He tried to remember what he had done early this morning. What had he done? His heart pounded with excitement. His hair prickled. He had—oh, yes, he had suggested that Rajin be called to help Jawab. Yet no one had called him—no one at all.

"Who called you?" Pakoo was asking in a severe voice.

"No one called us," Uncle Sobat answered. "All last night I couldn't sleep." He laid his hand on his brother's shoulder.

"I felt concerned about Saksee. He got a rather late start and his load was heavy. I wondered if he got home all right. I thought maybe one of you might be sick. I asked Rajin to come up with me this morning."

Pakoo was still sullen. "You can see for yourself that we are both well."

Then a sound came from the chief's house. It was a groan of agony. The two men started and looked toward the window of the house.

"Who's that?" Rajin asked with an expression of alarm and sympathy on his face.

Pakoo said nothing, and Saksee dug his toes into the grassy sod and looked at them.

"Is someone sick in the chief's house?" Uncle Sobat gave his brother a little shake. "Tell me—is the chief down with the fever again?"

"It is Jawab, the chief's son," Saksee found his voice at last. He looked straight into the eyes of the teacher. "He had a fight with his father early this morning before daylight and his leg is hurt."

"But that's impossible!" Uncle Sobat exclaimed. "The chief almost worships his son. He wouldn't hurt him for anything! Come, tell us the truth."

"They had been drinking quite a lot," Pakoo began to explain. "The chief is still drunk. He doesn't know yet that his son is hurt."

"Come, let's go and see what's wrong." Uncle Sobat led the way to the chief's house and Rajin followed him. Pakoo and Saksee lagged behind a little. They had just seen Kooning come out of his own door, and he was hurrying toward them with a look of astonishment and anger on his face. The teacher and Uncle Sobat had not noticed him. They were already calling in front of the chief's door. The chief's wife hurried to let them in. Her eyes were swollen with crying.

Kooning came down on Pakoo and Saksee like an angry bee. "What are they here for?" he screamed. "Who called them?" He waved his arms and spat in his rage. "How dare they bring their magic to this village?"

"Wait!" Pakoo took hold of the witch doctor's arm. "You are too quickly angry! No one called them. They just happened to come. They wanted to find out if Saksee got home all right. They didn't know about the chief's son until just now. They heard him moaning."

The small man jerked away from Pakoo's grasp and ran

Visitors 25

into the chief's house. The other two followed him. Saksee wondered what Rajin would do now. His mind was a whirl of wild thoughts. Had he really called the teacher? Early this morning when his heart had turned to the God of heaven and he spoke His name—had God been listening? Was that the reason Uncle Sobat couldn't sleep? Was God letting him know that there was trouble in the village of Broken Light? He felt as guilty as though he himself had made the long journey to Singing Water and called the teacher with his own voice.

Uncle Sobat and the teacher were kneeling by the mat where Jawab lay writhing and moaning.

"This is a dislocation of the hip," Rajin said. "How many hours has it been since he was hurt?" He looked at Pakoo.

Kooning screamed in fury. "You may go now!" he said, looking at Rajin with hatred in his eyes. His long yellow teeth clicked together. "Go! Go! We don't need your medicine in this village."

The noise of shouting roused the chief. He stirred in his sleep. He stopped snoring. He sat up on his mat and rubbed his eyes with his big hands. Then he saw his son. He saw the leg sticking out at his side. He heard the young man's groans. A look of horror crossed his face.

"What—what?" he muttered with a thick tongue. "What's the matter?" He staggered to his feet. "How did he get hurt?"

"The two of you had a fight early this morning and you threw him on the ground," Pakoo said without mercy.

At this Kooning began to dance about the floor in a frenzy of anger, swinging the small dried crocodile and screaming, "Go! Go!" He shook his clenched fist in Rajin's face.

Rajin still knelt by the injured man. He raised his eyes and looked at the witch doctor. "If the chief wants me to go, let him command me," he said. "It is his son who is hurt. If his leg is not straightened at once it will be impossible to do it. Even now it will be difficult."

The chief looked at Rajin with anguished eyes. "It is I who have done this terrible thing! It was the wicked spirits in the rice wine—the wicked spirits!" he moaned to himself. "Can you help us? Can you help us?"

Then Rajin asked Pakoo again, "How long has it been since he was hurt?"

"It was early this morning, before daylight."

"Four or five hours ago," Rajin said, biting his lower lip. "No time to lose. It is swollen already. You will have to help me.

Kooning stood watching for a moment. Now he ran outside the house, uttering wild shouts and imprecations.

Rajin looked around at Pakoo and Uncle Sobat. "You must help me. It will take three or four strong men to do this."

The chief's son was conscious now. He looked from one face to another with terror in his eyes. The pain of the dislocated joint was so great that he cried out with every breath. Beads of sweat stood out over his chest, his neck, his face.

Rajin took his hand. "My friend, you have been badly hurt. Now we are going to try to help you. It will cause much pain, but it must be done. You want your leg to get well, don't you?"

Jawab nodded his head. The teacher spoke again. "Be strong and brave and don't fight against us, even when we hurt you. Make yourself as limp and loose as you can. That will make it easier."

Then Rajin showed Uncle Sobat and Pakoo how to take hold of Jawab under his arms, pulling his shoulders away while the teacher pulled with all his strength on the crooked leg to straighten it. The chief stood over his son, calling out words of encouragement.

Visitors 27

Both Pakoo and Sobat were strong men, used to carrying heavy loads on steep trails for long hours, yet they braced themselves and pulled with all their strength; and at last the chief had to help them. It took the combined effort of them all. Saksee caught hold of Jawab's good leg and held it tightly. The young man tried to be brave and patient, but cry after cry of agony filled the house, and before the leg was pulled back into place, he became unconscious again. He lay limp and pale on his mat.

"Now we must splint it so it can't be moved or bent," the teacher said. "Bring me green bamboo."

The village people who had crowded into the room craned their necks to see what the teacher was doing. They were all eager to help. Some of them ran for the bamboo. The teacher sent others for soft old rags and strips of cloth. Rajin cut several strips of the green bamboo and smoothed them carefully with his knife. He bound them into a shell for the leg. It fitted tightly all around and extended from the hip to the foot. It was padded wherever it touched the flesh. It took a long time. Kooning had not come back.

Gradually the young man's face took on more color and his breathing came more quietly. The two visitors from Singing Water prepared to leave. No one had welcomed them to Broken Light. No one had spoken kindly to them. Only the chief had said in his deep trouble, "Can you help us?"

For that they had stayed. They had put Jawab's leg back in place. They had not prayed or sung songs or said the name of God. They did not need to. Saksee could hear it ringing in his mind. God was there in the chief's room where Jawab lay. God was in the path—in the house. This teacher brought God wherever he went, and he left God behind him too.

"Keep him quiet for a day or two, then prop him up as much as you can with the splint on; but he must not try to walk for a moon and a half—maybe two moons. See that you do as I tell you. Otherwise he will have much pain and trouble. Do you understand me?" Rajin spoke to the chief who sat sobbing beside his son.

"I will do as you say," he whispered in a broken voice.

"Feed him well and wash the rest of his body every day," the teacher said; and the two men started down the path leading out of the village of Broken Light.

Saksee stood in the door of his father's hut and watched them go. He was glad when they disappeared in the lower jungle. He felt uncomfortable and sad about the whole affair. He wanted time to think and to try to understand.

Did God really know about the chief's son being hurt? Was God there through the night while they were dancing and drinking? Did God see the fight? Was He sorry for the hurt man? Did He hear the desire of his own heart for the teacher to come? Had He really sent those two up the mountain, just in time? Who is God anyhow? Couldn't a person get away from Him? Was God going to come after him all the time now? Couldn't he even think without God knowing and answering?

He felt so troubled that he went to bathe at the spring. He scrubbed himself vigorously and let the cool water run over his naked body for a long time.

On his way back from the spring Saksee looked in at the chief's house to see how Jawab was doing. The old chief was feeding him rice gruel from a coconut shell.

"Does it still hurt?" Saksee asked as he knelt down to examine the neat splint Rajin had placed on the leg.

"Of course it hurts a lot!" Jawab answered in a weak voice,

"but nothing like it did before the strange young man pulled it into place. Who is he, anyhow?"

Then Saksee answered in a slow, unwilling voice, "He is the God-teacher from Singing Water."

CHAPTER 4

Preparing a Curse

IF Sakee could have been sure that God had left the village of Broken Light and was going down the mountain with Uncle Sobat and Rajin, it would have relieved his mind a great deal. As it was, he gloomed and glowered in the door of his father's hut. He knew that God was here—here in this village—in this house. Was there no way to escape from God?

Saksee resolved to throw himself into the work of his village and the old customs of his tribe. He would go every day to help his father in the rice field. He would keep watch over the growing rice, hardening now into ripe golden heads. He would work hard. In the evenings he would go to sit with Kooning and watch the old man make charms and prepare medicine and listen to his stories of the spirits and the folklore of his people.

The boy jumped up from his perch in the open door of the hut and began at once to carry out his resolve. He tried to do as much work as a man. He hunted in the jungle. He went to see Kooning every day. There must be no time for thinking about the God of heaven. It was difficult, because so many things brought the thought of God to his mind.

He remembered that Rajin taught the people of Singing Water how God made all the flowers, the birds, and the animals. Saksee couldn't look at a bright forest jay without wondering what God used to put that flashing color in his wings. Whenever he happened on a jungle flower and smelled its perfume, he wondered why God made it look and smell that way. It proved to be almost impossible to shut the thought of God from his mind.

The days passed quickly, filled with hard work. Each evening on his way to Kooning's house Saksee stopped to see Jawab. The chief's son was getting better. His mother had made some *kapok* pillows for him, and he was propped up as straight as he could sit with the splint on his leg. The old chief was often there. The father and son talked together a great deal. Jawab said the leg didn't hurt much any more.

Several times Kooning tried to remove the stiff bamboo splint the teacher had placed on the leg. Once he cut through some of the fastenings with his knife. The old chief fell into a rage over that.

"Let it alone!" he screamed at the witch doctor.

"But the leg will get well of itself without all this evil magic from Singing Water." Kooning was determined.

"Don't touch anything the teacher did!" Jawab warned him in a tone of severity. Then the two of them carefully mended the place where the bamboo splint had been cut.

"Who is this God of heaven?" Jawab asked Saksee a few days after the accident. "Isn't that God-teacher a worshiper of the God of heaven?"

Saksee had often asked himself this same question—"Who is the God of heaven?" He didn't know the answer, but he knew more about it than Jawab did. He had listened to Rajin talk about God for two moons.

"The teacher in Singing Water says that God lives up in the heavens beyond the stars in the sky; but His presence is everywhere. He made everything in this world."

Jawab sat on his mat and thought about this for a long time. "I would like to see God," he said at last.

"No one can see Him," the boy said. He knew that with the heart one could talk to God and hear Him too, but he was afraid to say such a thing. He wanted to get away from God. He hoped that when God saw how determined he was to cling to the customs and witchcraft of his people that God would go away and not trouble him any more. He left Jawab sitting there with a look of gladness on his face. He hurried on to Kooning's house.

"What are you making tonight?" Saksee asked the old man. Kooning was sitting in the middle of his floor on a mat. He was shaving some fresh bone into a little flat basket. On the mat beside him were little piles of hair—hair from some animal, a monkey perhaps. There were some odd-shaped twigs and a few dry seeds.

The old man looked at the boy a long time, as though he would read his very soul. Then, without answering, he went on with his work until he had a little pile of the bone shavings. Then he looked up again and searched Saksee's eyes.

"I think I can trust you," he said as he leaned forward on his mat. His small wrinkled face was very close. "Someday you will take my place as witch doctor for this village. It is right that I should show you everything. If you ever reveal what you see or hear in this room the demons will torture you, and you will surely die. I will tell you what I am making.

Saksee felt fear rising inside his body. He looked down at the piles of devil medicine on the mat between them and in the little basket. Then he looked again into the face of Kooning. He saw the snaggled yellow teeth, the cunning eyes, and the shrunken cheeks.

"I am making the medicine of madness!" the old man said. "If this medicine is placed near any person he will become confused in his mind and go mad."

Without wanting to or meaning to the boy shivered. "Why would you want to make that kind of medicine against anyone?" he asked.

"Can't you see? The chief's son is already taken in the heart by this foreign witchcraft. Since they put the bamboo on his leg and pulled him with their hands, he is bewitched. His heart is gone after that God-teacher."

Kooning bent again to his task. The thin shavings of bone fell silently from his knife. "Every day when I go to see Jawab he talks about the God of heaven and this teacher, Rajin, from Singing Water."

"Can you cure him with this medicine?" Saksee was terrified, but curious too. A disturbing thought came to him. Perhaps Kooning had some medicine prepared for him also.

"What about me?" he asked in a straightforward manner. "Why don't you make some medicine for me? I think about the God of heaven all the time. I can't help it. I don't want to, but I do. I think about Him and I hear Him talking in my heart."

Kooning looked at him in alarm. He drew out his small dried crocodile and waved it over the boy several times, as though to clear the air of some evil taint.

"Did the teacher lay his hand on you?" the witch doctor asked in a solemn voice.

Saksee thought back to the morning when he stood by the pool with Rajin—the morning he left Singing Water. "Yes, yes!" he shouted. "He did touch me. He laid his hand on my shoulder!"

The medicine man leaped up. His bone and knife clattered on the bamboo floor. He grabbed Saksee by the hand. "We will have to make strong medicine for you!" he screamed. "Strong medicine! We must make you forget! We must deliver your heart from this magic!"

"But I hate the God of heaven," the boy told Kooning. "I don't want to listen to Him. I don't want to know Him. I want to follow our own customs so I can become a witch doctor when I am older."

At this, Kooning calmed down a little. "I think it will go away," he said in a quieter tone of voice. "I think that if you come every day to talk with me and help me make medicine it will go away. Then you must help your father in the rice field all you can. Try to think about the spirits and how important it is to please them. I will make you a powerful charm. All these things will make it go away."

"I will do all you have said," the boy said, looking straight into Kooning's glittering eyes.

They both sat down on the mat again and were silent for a long time while the boy watched the old man mix the medicine of madness and put it into a small hollow joint of bamboo.

An uneasy feeling tugged at Saksee's heart. He was fond of Jawab. The chief's son was a fine young fellow. He would be chief someday. He was only four years older than Saksee. He had been through a terrible time of suffering. It seemed too bad to deliberately cause him more trouble.

Again the boy looked into the face of his companion. It was drawn into lines of cruelty he had never noticed before. Suddenly he felt a great longing to see Singing Water, to hold little Vee-Vee in his arms, to stand beside the sparkling pool below the village. It all came over him in a wave of longing, as when one is shut in a foul-smelling room and longs for a cool breath of fresh air. But the boy did not speak to Kooning about this thought in his heart.

"I suppose you must wait until the full moon," he said in a calm voice. "Doesn't all medicine take better when the moon is full?"

"Yes, that's right." Kooning still bent over his work. He was fastening a clever little top on the bamboo joint with a thong of rattan cut very thin. "I will wait till the full moon. You are a bright boy."

Saksee's heart gave a flutter of relief. He counted on his fingers, bending them over one by one. It would be ten days. He couldn't help hoping that something would happen—something that would deliver Jawab from the curse of Kooning.

He said, "Stay in peace," and went home to his father's house.

Pakoo was glad to see him. He was sitting by the oil lamp in the inner sleeping room. "You have been here for nearly three weeks," his father said. "You have helped me a great deal. Now the rice is ready to harvest. You know how bad the deer and the birds are this year. They will take our crop if we don't gather it in at once."

"I will help you, Father," Saksee said, throwing himself down on his own mat.

"Yes, I know you will help, but that is not enough. I want you to go early tomorrow morning to call your Uncle Sobat.

He always helps me harvest. There isn't a better rice-cutter in the mountains. You tell him to come as soon as he can—tomorrow, if possible."

"But, Father," the boy sat up. His heart was doing queer things. Now it was hammering in his chest. He put his hand over it to still its pounding. His father might hear! "Of course, I will go," he said.

When he lay on his mat that night he tried to think how the wish to go to Singing Water had come to him. He had been sitting there looking at Kooning. He had been thinking how cruel Kooning's face looked as he prepared the medicine of madness for the chief's son—then he thought of Singing Water. He remembered the face of Rajin as he worked over Jawab's dislocated leg. Then, like a bird flying in from the open sky, there had come that yearning desire.

This must be God again! Was God closer than the secret thought of his heart? He wriggled and squirmed and tried to find a comfortable position so he could sleep. God was here! The strength of God had never seemed so great. He stopped worrying about Jawab. A curious sense of rightness and rest flowed over him. He would go to Singing Water. He would see Rajin, Uncle Sobat, Aunt Gar, little Vee-Vee.

Saksee got up when the first streaks of rosy dawn lay along the mountains. He carried no burden, so the trip down the steep trail was easy. He flitted along like a forest creature. When he came hurrying into Singing Water Village and called before his uncle's door it was still early morning.

"Uncle Sobat! Aunt Gar!" he called in front of their house. "It is I, Saksee!"

Then without waiting for a welcome he pushed the door open and stood speechless at what he saw.

CHAPTER 5

Singing Water

THE boy stood in the door of his uncle's house, dumb with astonishment. The house was scrubbed and in perfect order. Even the clay stove had been cleaned and tidied. In the middle of the floor on a mat was a new book—a black one. It looked like the one Rajin used. Around it the family were gathered. They were kneeling just as Rajin had done that day at the pool. Even little Vee-Vee clasped her hands. She looked at her parents and did what they did. She smiled as though playing at an enchanting game. To Saksee it was terrifying.

Uncle Sobat looked up with a smile. "Come, we are just having family worship. Join with us, please."

Saksee could not move or speak. Uncle Sobat closed his eyes and prayed aloud to the God of heaven, asking Him to bless their home and give them rest and peace on this holy day. He asked God to bless Saksee and draw his heart to the good teaching. Then his voice broke in its earnestness. He spoke in low tones, "Dear Father in heaven, see my little Vee-Vee. Lay Your hand on her and make her like other children."

The boy still stood in the doorway, filled with consternation.

Could he be dreaming? He had been gone from Singing Water but three weeks, and now this change!

While Uncle Sobat knelt there on his mat with his rough hands folded and his eyes closed, talking to the God of heaven, the words of his prayer entered into the boy's mind and heart as though they were being driven in with a hammer—each one separately.

When the prayer was ended, the little family rose from their knees. Vee-Vee, who had been restrained by her mother's arm, now threw herself on Saksee in a whirl of delight. She was filled with the joy of seeing him again. So were Uncle Sobat and Aunt Gar. They made him sit down while they asked him of his father and the people of Broken Light; but most of all they asked him about the chief's son, Jawab. Was he getting better? Was he eating well? Was he sitting up a little now?

Saksee answered everything absent-mindedly. He was thinking so much about what he had just seen and heard that he forgot for the moment what he came for.

"Go, dip in the pool, my boy," his uncle was saying. "Have a good swim and then come to breakfast. The rice is already cooked."

"But, Uncle Sobat," Saksee remembered at last that he carried a message, "father wants you to come to Broken Light today to help us with the rice harvest."

Uncle Sobat smiled. "I thought that was what you came for. I have been expecting your father to call me; but I can't go today."

"This is the rest day of God—the God of heaven." Aunt Gar's face was shining. "Rajin has taught us about that, and now we are all worshiping on his Holy day. Almost everyone in the village is doing the same. This is the second time—the second week."

"You stay here and spend the rest day with us. We will have a fine time. We will go to the teacher's house and sing and listen to stories and tell one another what the God of heaven has done for us. Then tomorrow we will get up early and go to Broken Light and help your father with the rice harvest." Uncle Sobat had spoken. His face was lighted with pleasure.

It was already midmorning. The pool was empty. All the village folks had bathed earlier. Saksee was glad to be by himself so he could collect his thoughts. Had God arranged it so he would come here on this special day?

It looked as though his Uncle Sobat and Aunt Gar intended to follow this new teaching. The thing that grieved Saksee and made him a little angry was their great happiness. What right had they to be happy? They were forsaking the customs of their people. They were going after strange new things, yet there was gladness in their faces that he had never seen before.

Then, the house—it had always been dirty and disorderly, like all the other houses of the village. Now it was clean and well arranged. The black Book was in the middle of it. Did the written Word of God have power to enter a Dusun home and bring about this change?

The boy stripped off his sweaty garments and dived into the pool. The water had never seemed so pure, so inviting, so soothing. He swam for a long time, until he felt better.

When he returned to his uncle's hut breakfast was waiting. He saw that Aunt Gar had cooked a lot of rice. She smiled when she saw him peering into the big kettle.

"We do not cook on the Holy Day," she said. "I cooked everything yesterday."

Such a thing was unheard of. Everyone in all the villages cooked fresh rice at every meal. Still, it tasted good. He ate breakfast and followed the little family to the teacher's house.

It seemed to Saksee that he must have been away for months, the change was so great. The people came pressing into the teacher's house. They came from all over the village. They were clean and they looked about at one another with joy and affection. Kindness was in their faces. They did not talk after they entered the room. They sat with bowed heads until Rajin, in clean white clothes, stood before them and led the morning hymn.

The sweetness of their voices entered into Saksee. Although he could feel the gentle comfort of the place, he resisted. He felt it surrounding him and lifting him. He fought against this feeling, although it drew him with much power. He dare not give in to it! This was the poison Kooning had warned him about. It was taking hold of him. It would trap him and make him a prisoner. He knew that he should leap from his mat and leave the place; but he was so fascinated by the service that he could not tear himself away.

When Rajin spoke to the people it was to encourage them in their worship of God. He told them that God was in all their houses, hearing every word they said. "He knows what you are thinking. Even in the rice field and the jungle He is there. He is waiting to listen when you speak to Him. Most of all," the teacher emphasized, "God loves you, as a father loves his son."

The talking was not long, and the people listened with scarcely a sound to disturb the story. Then more hymns were sung. After this Rajin sat down on his mat and the people began talking one by one. They told of how they had come to know God, of how much they loved Him, of what He had spoken to them and done for them. Some of the stories were long. Some were only a few broken words, but everyone leaned forward on his mat and strained his ears to hear every word. Saksee could see that it was important—the most important thing in the world to these people.

The boy felt a strong urge to tell of his own experience on the mountain path the day he returned to his home village. He could tell them how God heard the unspoken word of his heart and sent help. He could tell of his desire for the teacher to come and help Jawab in his great trouble and how it had been answered. No, no, Saksee knew that he had no part in all this. It was not for him. He must stop his ears and his mind against this teaching.

Then he thought of Kooning and the medicine of madness he had prepared for Jawab, the chief's son. The thought seemed out of place in this company—like a whiff of foul breath from some decaying substance; yet he could not put it out of his mind, and it surprised him that here among these happy people worshiping the God of heaven he could think of the matter with such urgency. Perhaps he ought to tell Jawab about this worship. If Jawab should learn to trust in God—

Saksee remembered that one day Jawab would be chief of Broken Light Village. Would it be good to have a worshiper of God as chief? No, no. Such a thing must never be!

It was late afternoon when the people finished talking. They sang one more hymn and scattered to their homes.

While Aunt Gar was setting out the evening meal (these people do not eat in the middle of the day) Uncle Sobat sat on the mat with little Vee-Vee in his arms. Her black hair was neatly combed and braided. Two little bits of red rag were entwined into the ends of her long pigtails. She looked up, smiling into her father's face. But Uncle Sobat did not see her.

He seemed to be looking beyond the child into some far place. His face was thoughtful, not sad but filled with longing.

Saksee studied his uncle's face. He knew what Uncle Sobat was thinking. He remembered the words spoken to the God of heaven this morning in this same room. "See my little Vee-Vee. Lay Your hand on her and make her like other children."

Saksee sat quietly there in the neat room. He tried to collect his thoughts again. Yes—he had no doubt about it now—the God of heaven had heard his unspoken wish to come to Singing Water, and God had arranged it so he would be here at his uncle's house on this holy day.

The God-teacher had told them that nothing was too hard for God. Rajin was full of stories about deaf and lame and blind people—even lepers—who had been made perfectly well again by the word and power of God.

The boy pondered this in his heart. In all his life he had never seen a deaf or lame or blind person made well by any kind of witchcraft known in their villages. But now this teaching had come. Could such things happen? He knew that God was here in Singing Water—in this very house. He could feel the breath of God about him. Yes, God was in every house in this village, watching, listening, and loving—in Broken Light too.

Then Rajin called in front of Uncle Sobat's door. He came to ask about the chief's son. Saksee gave him a full report; but he did not reveal that Jawab's heart was turning toward the God of heaven.

"I think when the two of you go up to Broken Light tomorrow I will go with you. I want to see for myself that the young man's leg is healing properly," Rajin said.

The teacher didn't ask Saksee about himself. He didn't say

anything about God; but the words were there, unsaid, unasked, unheard except by the heart. The boy was glad when the teacher left, for there was a pressure behind his lips to reveal the secret Kooning had entrusted to him—the secret about the medicine of madness he had prepared for the chief's son.

There was a voice inside him that called, "Tell Rajin! Tell Rajin! Tell him to make the medicine of his God strong for Jawab!" But Saksee knew that he must not do this. He could not tell such a secret and live.

Saksee knew that someday he would be the witch doctor for the village of Broken Light. Kooning was his teacher now—not Rajin. Still the voice called—sometimes loudly, sometimes softly.

Early the next morning Saksee said good-by to his Aunt Gar and little Vee-Vee. Then he went with Sobat and Rajin up the mountain toward the village of Broken Light.

CHAPTER 6

The Trusting Heart

IT was late in the morning when Saksee with Uncle Sobat and Rajin climbed the last steep stretch of trail and entered the village of Broken Light. After bathing at the spring they went to the chief's house. Pakoo went with them.

"Where is Kooning?" Saksee asked his father. "Is he here in the chief's house?"

"He left early yesterday," Pakoo said. "I saw him go. He has not yet come back."

Jawab greeted them with warm words of welcome. With outstretched hands and grateful tears the chief's wife thanked them for their kindness to Jawab. The old chief rose from his place beside the young man's mat and received them with respect.

Jawab fixed his eyes on the teacher and said, "I am so glad you have come. My leg doesn't hurt much now. I want to know more about the God of heaven."

At this Rajin's face brightened with some inner light. He took the young man's hand in his own for a moment. Then he knelt to examine the leg.

"I can see that you are much better," he said. "You have

kept the splint in place. I think your leg is going to heal and you will be able to walk again; but it will be at least another moon. You must be patient and wait."

"Will I be able to come to Singing Water?" Jawab asked.

"Yes, I'm sure you will make many trips to Singing Water. It is possible that the hurt leg may always be a little shorter than the other one; but I'm certain that if you are patient and careful you will climb the mountain trails again, and you will go to the jungle to cut the big trees and plant the rice and hunt the wild deer."

"I want you to tell me about the God of heaven," Jawab said, and again Rajin's face glowed with that inner light.

"God is great and good. He made all the things we see—the trees, the plants, the rice, the moon and stars, and all the living creatures. And people, too. Then, of course, He made many things we can't see, such as the wind, the perfume of the flowers, and the kindness in the heart. God made everything in this world for us, so we might find food and homes and happiness, too, for ourselves and our friends."

The old chief grunted his approval, and his wife came to sit on the floor of the room just inside the door, where she took up some basket weaving and listened to all that was spoken.

"The God of heaven is strong and He loves us all. He is able to take care of us, so we need not be afraid."

The people who had crowded into the chief's house on that day when Jawab's leg was pulled back into place now came one by one and sat on the floor of the room, listening to the words the teacher spoke.

At last the chief spoke. "The witchcraft of our medicine men—what about that?"

Saksee was startled. He remembered the medicine of

madness that Kooning had prepared. Did the chief know?

"No witchcraft has evil power when the heart trusts in God," Rajin answered, still kneeling on the mat and looking straight into Jawab's eyes. "No matter what spells or devil magic are made, they will come to nothing and be harmless when the heart trusts in the God of heaven."

"I trust in the God of heaven," Jawab said in a quiet voice. "I have heard Him calling in my heart ever since the day you came and pulled my leg back into place."

"It is the loving-kindness of God that calls us and draws us to Him," Rajin said with a smile.

Saksee's mind bubbled with excitement. Surely Rajin must know about the devil medicine. But how could he know? Only two persons in all the world knew of it. The boy was pricked in the heart and a dark burden settled down on him—the weight of his dreadful secret.

They left the chief's house and went back to Pakoo's hut. By the time they had eaten rice it was time for Rajin to go back to Singing Water.

"While you are here," Rajin said to Uncle Sobat as he was leaving, "go and talk with Jawab every day. Teach him how to pray."

Then Rajin hurried alone down the mountain.

"There are many people waiting to talk with him," Uncle Sobat explained, "and there are many sick ones to be visited."

Saksee looked at Uncle Sobat and saw the same brightness in his face—the brightness of God that Rajin carried everywhere. It worried him. Now this teaching had taken hold in Broken Light too. The chief's son had said openly that he trusted in God. Could it be true that the medicine of madness would have no power against him now?

Saksee longed for some quiet place where he could think. His thoughts were almost more than he could bear. But the rice must be harvested. They went to the rice field. Everyone worked hard that afternoon. All that week they toiled with all their strength from daylight till dark; but when evening came and they could no longer see to work, Uncle Sobat bathed, put on clean, fresh clothing, and crossed the narrow distance between the two houses. There he sat with Jawab, and they spoke of God and the new teaching.

"Come along with me," Uncle Sobat would call to Saksee. "You have worked hard today. You deserve a little pleasure. Let us go to Jawab and talk with him."

Then in spite of himself Saksee would be persuaded to go. So he listened while Uncle Sobat told Jawab more and more about God and taught him to pray.

"Remember that God is your Father," Uncle Sobat said in an earnest voice. "You can talk to Him as you do to your father, the chief. He is right here—as near to you as I am. He has more power than any man. He can do anything He wants with people's bodies and minds and hearts."

"Is there anything God can't do?" Jawab asked.

"Well, yes, there is one thing He doesn't do—He could, but He has never done it. He doesn't make people do what He wants them to do. He doesn't force them to do anything."

The chief's son was silent for a little while as he thought about all these things. Then, before he could ask more questions there was a voice calling in front of the house. A moment later Kooning stood at the door of the inner room. He stared at them. The old witch doctor looked tired. His face was lined with sweat and dust. He must have been on a long journey. Surely it could not be for any good purpose. The boy felt sick at heart.

Kooning looked at Saksee—a long keen look. The boy knew the meaning of that look. The witch doctor was searching his face to discover if there was any turning in him toward the God of heaven. Saksee returned the look with a full open stare that was meant to say, "I am still standing fast for the old customs of our tribe."

Then Kooning stepped to the boy's side and placed a little package in his hand. Saksee turned it over and over in his curiosity. It felt hard. It was wrapped in a soft dried leaf. There was no time to open it now.

The witch doctor looked at Uncle Sobat. Anger came up in his eyes. His hands twisted together in a gesture of violent displeasure. Jawab looked at him and smiled.

"Come, sit down with us," he invited Kooning. "Sobat is telling me some wonderful things about the God of heaven."

Then Kooning exploded in fury. "Those who forsake the ways of their ancestors can expect nothing but evil fortune. Calamity will come. The spirits will have their revenge."

There was a look of such cunning and cruelty on the old man's face that Saksee shuddered. He knew what Kooning had prepared for Jawab. It was only a few days now till the full moon. A sickness clutched the boy's stomach. Only the fear of death had kept him from revealing the secret in Singing Water. He still feared the evil spirits. He was still in their power; but he was coming to care more and more for Jawab.

Now another thought struck him. Perhaps Kooning would prepare some terrible curse for Uncle Sobat. It was plain to see that he hated everyone connected with the God of heaven. Then what would happen? Would the new magic protect him?

The witch doctor stood looking at them all with rage and hate in his face. Then he left the house without more words.

Saksee found in his terror that now his sympathies had shifted from Kooning to his victims. Saksee had been in favor of keeping the new teaching out of the village and holding to the old ways of the Dusun tribe; but now was his heart changing? And so soon after he had promised Kooning with his eyes? What could be happening to him?

He knew that in spite of the assurance he had just given the witch doctor, in his inner self he longed for the gladness and peace of his Uncle Sobat and the calm childlike trust of Jawab. As it was, he had neither. He had only a small package in his hand. Suddenly he knew what it was—the charm! Perhaps Kooning had made the long, tiresome trip just to get that charm. The conflict of thoughts that stormed his mind was almost unbearable.

Then he saw his Uncle Sobat looking at him with a steady gaze. "Do not be frightened by anything Kooning threatens or by anything he does. God is able to take care of everything!"

Alone in his room Saksee opened the little package and looked at the charm. It was a little hand carved out of the breastbone of a bird. The color of the bone was red. He fastened the charm around his neck. Now this would certainly help. He felt better already. Now perhaps he could forget about God and not be troubled by thoughts of the new witchcraft.

Through the next few days they worked hard. Saksee slept with his charm around his neck. Often in the night he reached for it and held the hard little bone hand in his own. It seemed to help.

When the sixth day came the harvest was not yet in. One large field remained to be reaped.

"I will go back to Singing Water today," Uncle Sobat said. "I must spend the rest day in my own house. Why don't you both come with me? We can have a fine time together. Then we will return the day after tomorrow and finish the harvesting."

"No," Pakoo said. "I am afraid of what is happening in Singing Water and I don't want Saksee to go there any more."

"But you must not be afraid of God. He is good. He loves us. We need to know Him. It makes our life clean and happy."

"I know—I know, my brother," Pakoo smiled a scornful smile. "For you it may work out all right. But we will stick to the old ways."

CHAPTER 7

A Message for Uncle Sobat

IN spite of his disapproval of Uncle Sobat's new way of life, Saksee felt empty when he had gone. Loneliness filled the little hut. The mats lay on the floor where the three of them had slept. He stood in the middle of the room feeling as though something important had gone from the house.

"We must work hard today," his father said. "It will take us three or four days to reap that last field. I'm not sure Sobat will come back."

They worked hard that day and the next; but in spite of his new charm Saksee couldn't help thinking about the rest day down in Singing Water. He pictured in his mind how Rajin's face would look when Uncle Sobat told him how Jawab's faith and trust in the new magic was growing, and how Kooning's hatred increased every day. He could see the people gathered in the teacher's house and he knew the hymns they would be singing. He knew that after the morning hymn and the teaching they would sit around Rajin's big front room telling all that had happened to them during the week.

In the deep places of his heart he longed to be with them;

yet his mind rejected the thought with anger. He held the little carved-bone charm in his hand. How long would it take this little piece of bird bone to drive the thought of God from his mind?

He wondered whether Uncle Sobat would come back. No one had asked him to. In fact, his leaving the house had been rather unpleasant. But Uncle Sobat did come back early on the morning after the rest day. He was full of excitement about something the teacher had told them in their worship period the day before.

"You know," he said with a glowing face, "the teacher read to us from God's Book, and it says that if we have trust like a grain of mustard seed, we can ask what we will of God and He will do it."

He drew out a folded paper and opened it with great care. Inside the paper were tiny orange-colored seeds.

"Mustard seeds," Uncle Sobat explained. He held them out for Pakoo and Saksee to see. "The teacher, Rajin, gave them to me. He got them from the Chinese gardener at Inanam down at the foot of this mountain. He showed them to us all yesterday. He gave every family a few to plant, so we can understand better about the mustard seed and trust in God."

Mustard seed—mustard seed! Saksee had seen the Chinese mustard and eaten the leaves for greens. The plant was commonly used as a vegetable by the Chinese; but he had never seen the seeds before.

"The kingdom of God and His Word are like these seeds," Uncle Sobat was saying. "A little seed gets into a person's heart. It begins to grow, and soon there is a big trust in God." Then his face shone with joy.

"You see, we need only a little trust to receive what we ask for—" His thoughts seemed to wander in far places. "But that tiny bit of trust must have life in it—life like these little seeds."

Then Uncle Sobat divided the seeds in his hand into two portions. He gave half of them to Saksee. "Plant them today in the garden. See what they will do." He wrapped the other seeds in the paper again and tucked them into a pouch at his belt.

The boy took the small seeds into his hand and looked at them. All the way to the rice field he held them, and he planted them under Uncle Sobat's direction at the edge of the clearing near the rice field, where they had prepared a vegetable garden.

The last of the rice was gathered that day. They all worked hard, and it was late when they had washed and eaten. When Uncle Sobat went to talk with Jawab, Saksee said he would go to bed because he was so tired. The boy knew that Uncle Sobat would tell Jawab all about the mustard seed. He had been thinking about it all day. He tried to get it out of his mind, but it stuck there. Had God known of his desire to be in Singing Water yesterday and sent him these little seeds? It seemed quite probable.

In spite of himself he kept wondering what would be his most urgent request if he came to trust in God as did Uncle Sobat and Jawab. He could have anything he wanted from God if his trust was as big as a grain of mustard seed. He thought of several things he would like to have. He lay on his mat, wrapped in deep thought.

When his uncle returned he had not yet slept. He saw him come into the room and lie down on his mat. The moon was bright. It would soon be full! Then Saksee knew for certain what was the most urgent request of his heart—the medicine of madness! Let it come to nothing and be harmless!

Of course, Saksee knew that he had no right to make any request of God. He was against God. He was all for the old customs—the charm! The charm! He felt for it, and with it folded tightly in his hand he slept.

It was still dark outside when Saksee was wakened by his Uncle Sobat calling in a voice of wonder and delight, "I will have my wish! I will have my wish! My little Vee-Vee will hear and speak. She will be like other children!"

Saksee and his father sat up, rubbing their eyes and peering into the darkness to see what had happened.

"You worked too hard in the rice field, brother," Pakoo said gently. "You are dreaming. Go back to sleep and rest. It is not near morning yet."

"No, no!" Uncle Sobat was lighting the coconut-oil lamp. "No, no! I must not sleep more this night. I must tell you! It was a man! He looks like a God-teacher, but he is big and tall, much bigger than Rajin. He was dressed all in white and he told me that my prayer is heard. God will make it as I have asked!" Uncle Sobat was too excited to sit down. He danced about the little oil lamp on the floor like a joyous child.

"Man, that is impossible!" Pakoo stood up. His face became stern. "We have seen many people in our tribe who were born without hearing and without words. None of them ever came to be any different. Don't be a fool! This is madness!" Pakoo took hold of his brother and shook him as though he would jerk the foolish notions out of his head.

Then he spoke more quietly. "Be content to have Vee-Vee as she is. She is healthy and strong. She is a good child. She will learn to work and help you when she is older."

But Uncle Sobat paid no attention to anything they said.

A Message for Uncle Sobat

He continued to repeat again and again, "My little Vee-Vee—she will be like other children!" The light on his face was like nothing they had ever seen before. Their words fell around him like dead leaves on the forest floor.

When the first faint streaks of dawn filtered through the coconut tree outside the window, he prepared to leave.

"I must tell Vee-Vee's mother! I must tell Rajin!" He flew out the door and down the mountain path like a winged creature.

Saksee stood with his father in the door of their hut and watched him go. He disappeared among the jungle trees below the village. The sun had not yet reached the rim of the mountain, but the freshness of early morning lay over everything. The boy looked at his father.

"He really believes it!" Pakoo said more to himself than to Saksee.

"And I'll not be surprised if it happens," the boy cried.

His father looked at him in alarm. "It has never happened among our people. It never—"

Saksee interrupted him, "The God-teaching never came among us before."

It was still so early in the morning that Jawab would probably not be awake yet. Still Saksee hurried over to the chief's house and called in front of the door.

"You are early this morning," Jawab said, rubbing his eyes and yawning. "Where is your uncle? Has he gone back to Singing Water already?"

"He has gone," Saksee said in an excited voice. "He ran down the hill like a mountain deer. He saw some kind of big God-teacher in the night, and the God-teacher told him that his little girl will speak and hear."

Jawab turned on his mat and gasped in surprise. "Did he

really hear and see such a thing? What do you think it means?"

"Oh, I'm sure he really saw the man and heard what he said. You know, he grieves so much because Vee-Vee can't hear or talk. He asks God every day to make her like other children."

"Do you think it will come true?" The chief's son sat propped up on his pillows with parted lips and wonder in his eyes. Saksee thought he saw some of the brightness of the God of heaven about him, too.

"I know the God of heaven is strong. He could make Vee-Vee hear and talk, I'm sure. Such a thing would not be too hard for Him," Saksee admitted unwillingly.

"You don't think Kooning has made some devil medicine against him and he has gone crazy?" Jawab asked.

"Oh, no, no!" the boy's heart leaped with terror. "No, surely it couldn't be that! Kooning says the devil medicine makes people confused and sad and sick, grieved and hopeless."

They both sat and thought about it, and Saksee's secret trembled on his lips; but he choked it back—not now, not now! It was too dangerous. He knew that Uncle Sobat had never been healthier or happier in all his life. It couldn't be the devil medicine.

Somehow every person in Broken Light Village heard of the wonderful thing that had happened to Sobat in their midst. They heard it that very day. It was talked of in the gardens, in the jungle, and around the oil lamps in the houses. Many opinions were given on the matter. Some said the poor man had worked too hard in the hot sun and without doubt was coming down with a heavy fever. Others said that the new witchcraft was driving him mad. A few were awed with the thought of the great promise Sobat had received, and amazed that a messenger from the God of heaven had appeared in the village of Broken Light. What would happen next?

Excitement ran through the village. Some of the people found excuses to go down to Singing Water on errands. They came back and reported that everyone in Singing Water knew about the big God-teacher who had appeared to Sobat; but the child was unchanged.

Kooning was in favor of getting up a big devil feast. "Let us drive this new witchcraft out of this village so the spirits will feel comfortable again," he urged, "otherwise we may expect some great calamity."

"But at our last devil feast Jawab was hurt, and because of that the teacher from Singing Water came here," Pakoo reminded him.

After much discussion it was decided that the matter of a feast could wait until they could see how these things would turn out. The chief was inclined to waver between the new teaching and the old customs. The situation was clearly out of hand, and Kooning gnashed his yellow teeth in rage.

CHAPTER 8

Call Rajin

As the days went by, Saksee thought more and more about Singing Water. He wondered what Rajin said when Uncle Sobat told him about the God-teacher who had appeared to him in Broken Light. He wondered what Aunt Gar had said. Most of all, he wondered whether Vee-Vee might at any moment become like other children.

Pakoo often looked at his son in a peculiar searching manner. Could he read his thoughts? The boy wondered. Finally, on the third day at noon he suggested a trip to the garden.

"It is time we gathered some of our vegetables," he said. "There may be some ripe coconuts too. We should go tomorrow and bring them in."

"Why can't we go today, Father?" the boy asked. Perhaps if they went to the mountain garden he might throw off these thoughts about Uncle Sobat and Singing Water.

Pakoo agreed that the sun was still high enough to go and still return before sundown, so they set off with two empty *bohongans* in order that they might be prepared to carry home whatever fruits of the garden were ready.

Saksee wore his new charm. Perhaps it would help too. If he could only stop thinking about God, everything would be as it used to be—no, not quite the same, because he could never go back to Singing Water. Still, it would be better than now.

The garden was close to the place where they had harvested the rice. They gathered a quantity of cucumbers, squashes, and gourds, as much as they could carry in one *bohongan*. They reserved the other *bohongan* for the coconuts.

"Now you go up this coconut tree while I mend the strap on your *bohongan*," Pakoo said to Saksee.

The boy took off his shirt and, dressed only in his short black pants, he climbed the tree. It was an old tree and so bent that it stuck out from the mountainside like a crooked finger. It leaned over so far that there was no trouble at all to sit at the top and poke at the nuts. With his foot Saksee pressed and pushed one coconut after another, letting them fall to the soft ground beneath.

It was pleasant up there under the great green fronds of the palm. The wind cooled his head and rumpled his hair. He sat for a long time enjoying the glorious mountain scene below him and the delicious air aloft.

His father's voice recalled him to his duty, and after pushing off a few more nuts, he scrambled down the tree, sliding the last and steepest portion of the trunk with his arms locked about the tree and the soles of his feet pressing the trunk on both sides. He squeezed tight against the rough bark with his naked chest and stomach.

A piercing scream tore the air. The boy slid to the ground and now lay on the grass rolling about in pain and calling, "Fire! Fire!"

His father ran to him and dragged him from the spot.

"Poison caterpillars!" he said. "They must have started to crawl up the tree just after you did. You slid right through them!"

Pakoo grabbed a handful of damp mud from under the old trees at the edge of the clearing. He daubed the mud on the boy's chest and stomach and the soles of his feet. In a few minutes the intense pain slackened a little and a feeling of numbness came over him. He stood up.

"Let's go home right away," he said.

"Can you carry the coconuts?" his father asked.

"I can try," the boy said through clenched teeth. He looked down at the redness that was changing to deep crimson over the part of his body that had brushed the caterpillars.

The two set out for home about a mile away, but before the journey was half over the boy fell to the ground. Pakoo carried him home on his back, leaving the two *bohongans* in the path. He called Kooning to his house at once and sent someone to bring in the *bohongans*.

When Kooning came into the hut Saksee was sitting on his mat moaning and squirming with pain, which was growing worse again. The witch doctor looked at him in alarm and hurried to bring his dried crocodile and all his other charms. He stood over the boy shouting.

"This is because the God-teaching has been in this house! Let this be a sign to you to leave Rajin and his medicine alone! Now I know that your heart has turned toward the God of heaven. This new witchcraft is like these poison caterpillars. In the end it will burn you! It will poison you!"

"Help me, Kooning!" the boy gasped. "Help me! Help me!"

"This will not kill you. Other people have suffered the same thing," the witch doctor said with a smug look. "I think this will be good for you. Perhaps now you will consider how you have offended the spirits. They are angry with you!"

Kooning shook his dried crocodile about the room a few more times and left the house.

The boy ran his hand along the burning surface of his body. It was all bumpy and felt like many large fat beans laid close together. Night had come now and the pain was almost unbearable. His whole body was caught up in such twisting agony that he could hardly move his legs. The stung places grew hotter and hotter, and they swelled with the poison. His head throbbed. His blood raged with fever. He called for water continually, and Pakoo sat by his side to give him long cool drinks from a joint of bamboo.

"Call Rajin—call Rajin!" the boy finally let the words burst from his dry lips in a shrill scream. "Call the God-teacher. He will help me!"

"My son," his father spoke gently, "perhaps this punishment has come to you because of the God-teaching in this house. Perhaps it is because Sobat was here."

The long hours of darkness were a nightmare of anguish. By morning the whole front of the boy's body was a mass of angry red bumps like the beginning of boils. His heart beat fast. His head burned with fever. Still Pakoo sat by the stricken boy, and Kooning spread the news through the village.

"The curse of the spirits has come to Saksee," the old man gloated. "Both he and his father have listened to the words of Sobat, and this is their punishment."

The news was brought to Jawab as he lay on his mat, and sadness filled his heart. He prayed aloud to the God of heaven.

"Oh, send the God-teacher—send the God-teacher to Broken Light today!"

The old chief heard the words as he ate his rice in the kitchen of his house. He left his food unfinished, and wrapping his dark garments about him, he hurried out the door.

No one saw him go. No one saw him return. The old man made the trip to Singing Water in less time than many younger men might have done. He delivered his message and took his time climbing the steep path home. Swifter feet than his were pressing the trail. Stronger hearts than his were touched by the urgency of his request.

When Rajin and Uncle Sobat entered the hut early that day Pakoo was astonished to see them. "Who called you?" he demanded.

"It is I who called them," the sick boy whispered. "They have come in answer to the desire of my heart." He managed a feeble smile and said, "I will be all right now. Rajin is here."

He lay in the inner room of his father's hut. His abdomen and chest as well as the soles of both feet were covered with boils, angry and inflamed. They were so close together that they seemed to run together into one mass of burning flesh.

"This kind of hurt is worse than anything else I know about," Rajin said as he knelt beside Saksee's mat. "I had it happen to me once—same way, too. I was sliding down a tree."

From his coat pocket he drew a folded paper and in it were some round white disks as small as one's finger tip. Uncle Sobat handed Rajin the water bamboo and he held it to the boy's lips. "Here, take a couple of these. It will help a little."

Saksee swallowed the two pills, and the teacher examined all the stung places—the boy's stomach and chest and the soles of his feet. His arms had not been stung. The only way Rajin could account for that was to suppose he had let go with his arms as soon as he felt the burning stings.

"Have you any coconuts?" the teacher asked Pakoo.

Pakoo pointed to the *bohongan* full of nuts they had gathered in the garden yesterday evening.

"Scratch the meat from two of them and press out the white milk. I need it."

Uncle Sobat grabbed two coconuts and hurried to find the coconut grater. In a few minutes he was back with the milk. The teacher dipped pieces of cloth in the coconut milk and laid them on the boy's burning skin. It felt easier at once, and a slow relief began to enfold Saksee. Then he slept.

That night Rajin sat with the boy all through the dark hours. It was Rajin's hand that poured water into his parched mouth. It was Rajin who kept the coconut milk on the cloths, which renewed and refreshed his body with their oily coolness. It was Rajin who put the white disks of medicine in his mouth twice during the night. When morning came the pain had diminished, but the teacher would not let him sit up. He propped his head on a bag of rice and fed him some soft gruel for breakfast.

The next day the thick clusters of boils were ready to open, and with great care the teacher pricked each one and drained it. After this the boy felt better than he had since the accident. The wet cloths were still laid on regularly; but now Uncle Sobat sat beside him while Rajin slept in the same room.

When evening came again the moon shone through the little window into the sleeping room. Saksee wakened during the night. The oil lamp was out. He knew that his father and Rajin were sleeping close to him. The moonlight was too bright, too piercing! It sickened him. What was it about the full moon? Why had he dreaded it so much? Slowly he remembered, and he cried out in anguish.

"The moon is full! The moon is full!"

Rajin leaped to his feet and knelt beside him. "Yes, the moon is full," he said. "Do not let it trouble you. God made the full moon. It is beautiful!"

"But this night—this night of the full moon—Kooning has laid the medicine of madness against the chief's son!"

The two men were now thoroughly awakened. It was still dark. They lit the oil lamp and looked at each other with apprehension in their faces. The boy moaned in distress.

"Are you in pain?" Rajin asked him.

Saksee shook his head; but he sat up and rocked back and forth on his mat in an agony of grief.

"It is Jawab! Jawab!" he cried, looking from one face to the other. "It is my fault—all my fault! I should have told you."

"But Jawab is all right. Nothing is wrong with him. What do you mean?" Rajin laid his hand firmly on the boy's shoulder. "Perhaps you should tell us all about it. Then you will feel better."

"Kooning has made the medicine of madness against Jawab this night. It is already done. Nothing can stop it! Nothing can turn it aside!"

The teacher's face relaxed into a slow smile. "Your Uncle Sobat is sleeping in Jawab's room tonight. He is lying on a mat right beside him. He went over there to talk and decided to stay the night. I'm sure no devil medicine will have any effect on Jawab or anyone else in that house. God is there."

"You see," Saksee's father spoke, "there were only three mats here, and Jawab has been begging Sobat to sleep over there. He slept there last night, too; but you were too sick to know about it."

So here was God again—God! He had known about this

night of the full moon all along. He knew how to protect Jawab—He arranged for Uncle Sobat to be sleeping beside him. He knows how to work out all things to protect His people. It came with clear conviction. The burden he had carried for weeks lifted. He took the charm from around his neck and gave it to Rajin.

At that moment a sound outside startled them all. It was the sound of running feet.

CHAPTER 9

The Angel

THE three people who sat in the circle of light from the tiny coconut-oil lamp listened with startled surprise as the sound of running feet came closer. Then they heard shouts of joy. They recognized the voice. It was Uncle Sobat. He burst in the door and stood before them. Even in the frail light from the oil lamp they could see that something extraordinary had happened to Uncle Sobat. His face was transfigured with wonder and ecstasy.

Before anyone could ask why he came, he told them in a voice of pure delight, "He came again! He came again!" He choked with the overwhelming joy of it. "He came again!"

"Who came?" they all asked.

"The big God-teacher from heaven!" he pointed upward. "He came again. He told me that my little Vee-Vee will hear and speak. She will be like other children on the day I am baptized!"

"Sit down, my friend, and calm your heart." Rajin took him by the arm. "Sit here by me and let us talk a little about this God-teacher you have seen. Were you asleep when he came?"

Uncle Sobat was still too excited to sit down. He stood

looking at them with that glow of pure glory in his face.

"Jawab and I talked for a long time last evening, and we were tired and very happy. We both went to sleep. Then the big God-teacher came and wakened me. He laid his hand on my shoulder and he said, 'Your prayer is heard. Your little child will hear and speak on the day you are baptized.'"

"Did Jawab see the young man or hear the voice?" the teacher asked.

"No, no! I woke Jawab and told him. I woke the chief and his wife. I told them all. I ran here to tell you. My heart is full of great joy!"

Then Rajin spoke slowly with great earnestness as he said, "This is a wonderful thing! When you told me about the first time the young man appeared to you I thought it might be a dream. You see, your heart longs so much for Vee-Vee to hear and speak that it is possible you might dream about it from wanting it so much." The two men stood in the middle of the room. Rajin still held Uncle Sobat by the arm.

"Come, sit down. I want to ask you some questions," Rajin urged.

Uncle Sobat sat down and waited, but his face still beamed and they could see that his whole body was quivering with tremendous excitement and great joy. He looked at Rajin.

"Was this a dream?" Rajin spoke slowly and in a solemn tone.

"No, it wasn't a dream. I was asleep when the young man laid his hand on me. Then he spoke to me and wakened me. I was as I am now."

"Then God must have sent His angel to talk with you, and the God-teacher you saw is one of God's angels."

"You did not teach us anything about angels," Sobat said.

"There are many things I have not yet taught you. There is so much to know about God. The angels are God's messengers. There are thousands and thousands of angels—more than can be counted. They are very strong. They go everywhere doing errands for God. Sometimes they have appeared to people as young men."

Uncle Sobat clapped his hands with gladness. "It is one of God's angels I have seen. God sent him to me—to me!"

Then Rajin put both his hands on Uncle Sobat's shoulders and turned his face toward the light so that he might look into his eyes. "I believe, now, that God sent His angel to bring you this good news. See that you never doubt it; for it will surely come to pass. It will be as the angel has said."

Then Pakoo spoke up. "Teacher, what does it mean to be baptized? What did the angel mean when he said that on the day Sobat is baptized Vee-Vee will hear and speak?"

"When a person has learned to love and trust God, when he has learned to talk to Him as a Father, when he has decided to do all things to please God, then he is baptized. He goes down into the river and I lay him under the water for just a moment. It is a sign that the old heathen life is finished and buried like a dead thing. Then the man rises out of the water again to a new life of holiness for God."

"When will this be done?" Pakoo asked in a low voice.

"We have not yet set a day; but it will be at least one moon from now. It will be on God's holy rest day. There are a number of people in Singing Water who will be baptized."

The rest of the night passed in earnest talk and none of them remembered the curse of Kooning or the devil medicine he had made against Jawab.

When the light of morning filtered into the hut, Saksee

was much better. That day Rajin opened the boils again and drained them. The boy rested. His mind was clear now. He could think about the wonderful thing that had happened—first in this very room, then last night in the chiefs house. An angel—a messenger of God—had been in this room. Was he still here? The pain was almost gone.

A clear image of Vee-Vee came before his mind. He saw the way she smiled at them with a questioning look in her eyes and her head bent a little like a bird. He remembered how often he had held her in his arms and shouted her name over and over again; yet she never knew nor heard. Could it be possible that she would be changed?

Uncle Sobat and his father left the hut. It was an hour before they came back. He did not talk with Rajin. They both sat thinking of all that had happened the night before. When Pakoo came back he was alone.

"Did Uncle Sobat go home?" Saksee asked.

"Yes, he went home to Singing Water. But first he went to every house in this village and told the people that God's angel had talked with him last night and that Vee-Vee will be like other children on the day he is baptized."

Sakscc could close his eyes and see Uncle Sobat hurrying down the steep trail. He would run to his house. He would tell Aunt Gar while he held Vee-Vee in his arms—his little child who would be like other children in another moon—another moon. Saksee drifted off to sleep.

When the boy woke up he asked for Rajin. His father sat beside him with a dish of hot rice. "You should eat this now. You are thin and weak. Come, take the rice!"

"But where is Rajin?" Saksee insisted, as he took the food in his hand.

"Rajin has gone to talk with Jawab. The chief sent for him. He will talk with them and eat there. Then he will come back."

"Father, Father, do you believe that the angel of God came to Uncle Sobat? Do you think it will be as he said?"

"My heart is rocking back and forth like a tall tree in the wind. I don't know what to think," the older man said as he scratched his head and sighed.

It was late afternoon when Rajin returned. The chief was with him. The whole village was astir with excitement over what had happened the night before. They began to crowd into the little room where Saksee lay on his mat. They talked in excited tones. Some were angry. Many were curious. A few were happy. Kooning was not with them.

"Go to your houses," Rajin told them. "Tonight we will gather in the chief's big council room, and I will tell you about the God of heaven and His angels."

Then the people went away. Pakoo and Rajin sat down close to Saksee's mat. Rajin took a small bamboo container out of his shirt pocket. He opened it, and Saksee almost leaped off his mat. It contained the shavings of bone, the hair and the sticks, and the other devil medicine Kooning had mixed and mingled with his curses. He had prepared it for Jawab. Now Rajin held it calmly in his hand. No Dusun would have willingly touched it.

"The chief found this hanging under the floor directly beneath Jawab's mat," he explained. "That's why he called me over to his house. He was very frightened. But don't be afraid of it. This medicine is harmless to those who trust in God. Jawab trusts in God."

Then Rajin looked at them both with a smile on his face. "Jawab is going to be baptized too. I think he will be able to walk in another moon. If he can't walk to Singing Water we will carry him."

Then the teacher dressed the boy's boils and made him comfortable for the night. When he had finished, the chief came to tell him that many people already were gathered in the council room. Rajin went to talk to them. In a few minutes Saksee heard the teacher's voice raised in a familiar hymn. He was teaching the people of Broken Light to sing. Saksee was quiet. The pain of his stings and the distressing boils was almost gone. To the melody of Rajin's song he drifted off to sleep.

It was early morning when he wakened. He lay on his mat—thinking. He looked down at his chest. It had turned a bluish color and it itched. Rajin said it would be so when it began to get better. Saksee wondered what would have happened to him if Rajin had not come. Now he thought about God. Who is God? The question pressed his mind. He is a great Father. That much he knew. He is a skillful Healer. He has angel messengers–thousands of them; so He must be a great Rajah also. He is here in this room. It is not possible to get away from God. He—Saksee—had fought God for three months.

He thought of the mustard seed. He wondered whether the seed had sprouted. He resolved that as soon as he could walk he would go to the garden clearing to look at the place where the seeds were planted. They should be growing by now. He would see for himself how a mustard seed can grow. The Word of God—the thought of God—is like a mustard seed. The tiny living thing inside the seed makes it shoot forth and grow. The Word of God is living too.

When the two men wakened, Saksee called to them. "Father, Rajin." He raised up on his mat. "Could you carry me to the chief's house? I can lie on my mat there beside Jawab and we can talk."

Rajin laughed. "You are much better! I have been waiting for this request. We will take you now. Then I must go back to Singing Water. You don't need me any more."

The two men lifted the twelve-year-old lad easily and carried him to the chief's house. They laid him on a mat beside Jawab in the inner room, where he was welcomed by the whole family, and the chief's wife hurried to fix him a good breakfast of rice and fish.

Rajin ate with them, then saying, "Peace be with you," he left the village.

Pakoo went to attend to many duties that had been neglected since Saksee's accident. The chief went out too, and the chief's wife was busy carrying water and pounding rice. An atmosphere of peace filtered through the place—a sense of comfort and healing.

When Saksee studied Jawab's face he understood why the room seemed like a holy place. The chief's son was alive with happiness. It shone in his eyes. As soon as they were alone he spoke to Saksee.

"Do you know that Kooning hung the medicine of madness under my sleeping mat last night?" he asked.

"Yes, I know," Saksee said. "Rajin showed it to me." Then his heart overflowed and the words burst from him. "Oh, Jawab, I knew! I saw Kooning making the medicine! He told me the spirits would kill me if I told anyone about it!" He bowed his head and waited for Jawab's anger.

"Do not blame yourself," the chief's son told him. "I am sure I would have done the same thing a moon ago. God is leading us all to know Him and His power, but it comes slowly for us because we have been blind so long."

Then Saksee could raise his head again. "Weren't you afraid

when you saw the medicine?"

"When my father brought it up from under the house I was greatly surprised, but not afraid. God held my heart between His two hands, and I was safe. Kooning hates God, but he cannot hurt us."

"Does Kooning know that God was here last night? Does he know that the angel spoke to Uncle Sobat?"

"Of course he knows. Sobat told everyone."

"Does Kooning know that you are going to be baptized?"

"I think everyone in the village knows that, too," Jawab laughed. "It is possible that my father and mother may be baptized at Singing Water. We have told everyone. This is our day of gladness."

"I'm afraid Kooning will find some way to make trouble for you," Saksee said, leaning forward on his mat. "I think he will seek for some way to hurt you or make you sick so he can say that his curse came true."

At this moment there was a voice calling in front of the house. They both knew it was the witch doctor. He opened the door and came into the inner room where the two boys lay. He looked down at them. His eyes narrowed with savage cunning. He gazed at Saksee's naked chest—no more wet cloths on it now. He eyed Jawab's splinted leg as though a new thought had entered his mind. Then he left the room without saying anything.

As he walked away from the house a sound came floating back to the two who lay on their mats listening. It was the sound of demoniac laughter.

CHAPTER 10

Flame of Fury

FOR the next few days Saksee stayed in the chief's house. He was carefully tended by the chief s wife—Jawab's mother. Pakoo came to see him every day, and he continued to get better. It was a full week before he slept in his own house again, and even after he began walking about the village he still spent most of his time with Jawab. These two enjoyed talking, and Saksee was not yet strong enough to work.

A trader had come to the village of Broken Light the day after Rajin left. He was a half-caste, a Chinese-Malay. He was hunting for *kajang*. The people of Broken Light were skillful at making fine *kajang*. The palms whose leaves are used for that purpose were especially fine on that part of the mountain. The *kajang* is prepared by sewing palm leaves together into sheets. Threads of rattan are used for the sewing, and when the sheet is finished it may measure as much as a yard-and-a-half square. It is of double thickness. These palm-leaf sheets are used for many things—for walls of houses, roofs of temporary shelters in boats or gardens, booths at the outdoor market places, roofs of buffalo carts, and for covering anything that needs protection in that land of heavy rain.

The trader offered a good price for one thousand sheets of *kajang*. The village people were greatly pleased and set to work gathering the palm leaves, sewing them into sheets, and drying them in the sun. As the sheets were finished they were stacked under the chief's house, because it was larger than the other huts in the village and also because the trader held the chief responsible for filling the order. The men, of whom there were about thirty, gathered the leaves while the women did the sewing, drying, and stacking.

For days this had been going on, and while Saksee sat with Jawab in the room above, they could hear the rustle of the *kajang* sheets as the women worked with them under the house. The job was almost finished now.

Saksee looked down through one of the wide cracks in the bamboo floor. "They have filled it solid under half of the house," he said. "Now they are putting it under here, so we can't look down much longer. I wish I could go and gather palm leaves."

"I would like to go too," Jawab said, "but it will be another two weeks before I can begin to walk. Rajin said so." He looked down at his splinted leg with a frown.

Jawab tried to look down through the floor; but the splint on his leg bothered him, so Saksee kept him informed.

Kooning, who seemed to know the trader, was bustling about everywhere, overseeing the work and telling the women how to store the finished pieces. He appeared to have forgotten all about the God-teaching and his hatred toward it.

The two boys talked constantly about God and the coming baptism and little Vee-Vee. The day had been fixed now. It was to be three weeks from the next rest day. As the boys talked their interest grew, and their faith grew too.

"Why don't you get baptized too?" Jawab asked Saksee one afternoon as they sat together. "You believe in God."

"I believe that God is here. I have heard Him speak to me. I know He is powerful and kind; but my heart still flutters about like a bird in a net, struggling to be away. My trust is not quiet and sure like yours."

Jawab thought about this for a little while. "Does your heart long for God?"

"When I am in trouble—yes—my heart longs for God. But you long for Him at all times. That is why you are ready and I am not," Saksee sighed.

The boys knew when the rest day came. Rajin had shown them how to count the days and remember the seventh one. On this day they sat in the chief's house singing snatches of songs they could remember and talking about what they had learned of God's Word. The chief and his wife joined them and laid aside all work for that day. The *kajang* sheets were all finished. Tomorrow the trader would send coolies to carry them down the mountain to the market place at Inanam. They were all stacked in neat piles under the chief's house.

The sun was almost dowrn when Uncle Sobat called at their door and came in to greet them and sit with them.

"We thought someone from Singing Water should come to see you before the rest day is over," he exclaimed. "I will stay till tomorrow morning."

Then Uncle Sobat began telling them all that had taken place in his village this week and they told him all they had been talking and thinking about, and they asked him many questions.

"Why is it that no one is walking about the village? Is

everyone gone? It looked deserted when I came," Uncle Sobat said as he stood up and looked out the window.

The chief said, "The people have worked hard for several days gathering palm leaves and sewing *kajang*. They are tired. I suppose they are resting in their houses."

"I'm sure no one knows you are here," Jawab said, "or they would all be crowding in here to ask news of Vee-Vee and the baptism."

"I'm tired too," Uncle Sobat said, settling himself on a mat. "We will just have a quiet time here by ourselves, and if no one knows I'm here, that is good. We have much to talk about."

So the sun went down and the oil lamp was lit. Pakoo came over to see when Saksee would be coming home. He stayed for a little while and they all worshiped there, gathered around the lamp in the middle of the floor. Even Pakoo bowed his head and listened. Then Saksee and his father went home.

Uncle Sobat said he would sleep in the chief's house because he wanted to visit with Jawab a little longer.

That night it rained. The village slept. The sheets of mist and drizzle that shrouded the mountain hid all the stars, and there was no moon. Saksee listened to the gentle beat of the rain on the roof. Peace filled his mind. He slept.

It seemed to the boy that he had scarcely closed his eyes when he was wakened by the noise of many people shrieking from all over the village. It sounded above the patter of the rain. They were calling "Fire! Fire!"

Saksee's first thought was to question how anything could burn on a night like this. Both Pakoo and Saksee ran to the door and looked out. It was the chief's house! The roof was wet and black in the night. The stacks of *kajang* under the floor were burning with a fierce blaze that threw an eerie glow over the surroundings. The fire had already eaten through the floor. It was falling in!

"Jawab! Jawab!" Saksee screamed and started to dash out of the hut. But his father held him back.

"Look," he pointed to an approaching staggering figure. It was Uncle Sobat. He carried Jawab in his arms. They could see how excited he was.

"I saw! I saw—!" he began.

"Are you hurt?" Pakoo shouted at him.

"No," Uncle Sobat said. "Thank God we are not burned! I will put Jawab here in your house for a little while."

"Where is the chief? Where is Jawab's mother?" Pakoo screamed above the roar of the fire. "Are they in there—in that fire?"

"No, they aren't there," Uncle Sobat answered as he came up into the hut and put Jawab down on a mat in the inner room. "Someone came and called them. A boy came to the door and asked them both to come quickly."

"Doesn't the chief know that his house is burning?" Saksee stood in the door watching the fire.

"Oh, I'm sure he knows by now. The light can be seen all over the village, and the rain is less now. I thought only of getting Jawab out. In a minute more he would have been burned up. That fire was quicker and hotter than any I ever saw. He couldn't possibly have gotten out by himself."

The village people were running round the burning house in wild confusion. Pakoo and Sobat went out among them. Saksee stood in the doorway and watched. He told Jawab what he saw.

The building burned quickly, for it was made of bamboo and thatch and *kajang*. The piles of dry material under the floor were protected from the rain and they were tinder dry. They burned in a few minutes with a furious flame that nothing could resist. No one tried to do anything. They scampered about, screaming and babbling in surprise and fright. Then the old chief and his wife came hurrying up. They must have been at the far end of the village.

"My son! My son!" the chief cried in a mighty voice. He tried to dash into the burning ruin.

Many hands held him back. Jawab's mother began to wail and shriek. Then the wailing was taken up by the village women who did hot know what they were wailing about. Some of them had seen Uncle Sobat carry Jawab to safety; but most of them did not know whether Jawab was safe.

Uncle Sobat pressed through the weeping women and laid his hand on the chief's shoulder.

"Come! Come!" he said. "Jawab is safe. Let me take you to him."

The old man allowed himself to be led to Pakoo's house. When he saw his son sitting on the mat smiling at him he threw himself on the floor and sobbed like a child. "It is good! It is good!" he said. "The God of heaven has sent Sobat to save my son. From this day my heart will follow God!"

Jawab's mother stood beside him with big tears running down her cheeks. She felt of his face and hair. Jawab reached up and took one of her hands in his. "It's all right, Mother. I am not hurt at all. God sent Sobat to save me."

"Who was it that called you away from the house just before the fire started?" Pakoo asked the chief.

"It was a little lad—the little lad who lives in the farthest house down the mountain at the end of the village." The chief shook a trembling finger at Sobat. "You see, the boy told us that one of the people in that house is very sick and we must both come at once, even in the night and the rain." He sat down on the mat beside his son. "When we got there"—he looked around with dazed eyes—"when we got there no one was sick. They said it must be a mistake—the little boy made a mistake!"

"No! How could that be?" Pakoo's face was stern. "This is a strange thing! Did the little lad who called you see Sobat in your house?"

"No, of course not," Uncle Sobat spoke up. "I didn't say anything. Jawab and I had been talking. I just put out the lamp and lay down on my mat. Certainly no one knew I was there. If he had known—!"

"What do you think started the fire?" Pakoo took the chief by the shoulder in great excitement.

"Someone put fire in the *kajang* under the house," the old man said.

"It was Kooning. I saw him," Uncle Sobat said quietly. "It was he who set fire to the *kajang*. When the flames leaped up I saw his face. Then he saw me and ran away."

Fear and surprise struck the little group dumb when they realized Sobat had seen Kooning start the fire.

Then the chief stood up. "It was the witch doctor who had the boy call us away. He intended to burn Jawab alone there on his mat!"

"But the God of heaven had already sent Sobat into your house without any person in the village seeing him—" Pakoo began in a loud voice.

"He meant to burn Jawab because he loves the God of heaven. He wants to burn him because Jawab is going to be baptized and because the medicine of madness that was made against my son came to nothing and was useless!" The chief got more and more excited. He talked faster and faster, and lifted his voice higher and higher.

The people outside heard him and began to press in the door. Then the chief beckoned to them all to listen, and he explained to them what had happened and who did it and why. Exclamations of surprise and anger came from the company. Some wanted to go right then in the rain and hunt for Kooning and punish him at once; but the chief restrained them. He had calmed down now and could talk to them with authority.

"Go to your houses and sleep," he told them. "I will stay here in Pakoo's house. We can sleep in his kitchen. Tomorrow we will begin to gather materials for a new house. We will make it better than the old one and we will make one big room for the God of heaven, so we can worship there on His holy day."

CHAPTER 11

The Mustard Seed

IN the days that followed the burning all the people of Broken Light Village worked together to build a new house for their chief. This was not a long task, for a Dusun house can be built in a few days if the materials are on hand. It is made on a frame of poles. These the men cut in the jungle. Then the *kajang* walls and thatch roof are added. The materials are light and easy to work with. The village people who had cured bamboos brought them for the floors. Those who had stores of other supplies provided all that was necessary, and the work went forward rapidly.

Kooning had not returned or been seen about the village since the fire. His house stood open and his charms and other belongings were scattered about on the floor; but he had disappeared.

"I don't think he will come back," the chief said. "I think this new magic is too strong for him, and when he saw that Sobat had discovered his wickedness—"

"I think he will come," Pakoo said. "I think he will come sneaking in some dark night and take his charms. He regards them as of great value, you know."

By the time the new house was finished Jawab had started to use his leg a little. Rajin came to take off the bamboo splint at the end of seven weeks. He showed Jawab how to exercise his leg, and he fixed him a crutch that could be used until the leg became strong enough for walking.

Saksee was now entirely recovered from his terrible accident with the poison caterpillars. He was able to help with the chief's new house. The boy felt free and happy. He hoped that Kooning would never come back.

Now the coming baptism was the talk of the village. In a few more days little Vee-Vee would hear and speak like other children.

"Do you think it will come true?" they asked one another.

"We will go and see," they all agreed.

"If the God of heaven can make that child well after she has been deaf and dumb these six years, then He can do anything for any of us," someone said.

"The God of heaven can do anything for those who trust Him fully," Jawab told them.

Then Saksee remembered the grain of mustard seed. He would go now and look at the spot where the seeds were planted in the garden by the rice field. He would try to understand more of what Rajin had said about the grain of mustard seed. He had not been back to the garden since his recovery.

Fastening an empty *bohongan* to his back, the boy explained to his father that he intended to go to the garden to see if any fruits or vegetables were ripe for harvesting. Then he hurried off down the narrow path that led to the garden clearing a mile away.

Swinging along the mountain trail, Saksee thought about

God. He thought of God all the time now. Of course, other things sometimes crowded into his mind and the thought was pushed back; but it always came back, and the longing to know God became stronger and stronger. It was like bending a sapling over to gather fresh leaves from its crown. The sapling could be bent, but as soon as it was released, it flew back to an upright position, with its crown pointing toward the sky. In this way his heart might be bent to the right or the left, but it always came back to its true position—pointing toward God.

Saksee reached the jungle clearing. He saw that weeds and brush were growing fast in the rainy weather. He pressed his way through them to the spot where they had buried the tiny orange-colored seeds. There were plants there. They had grown green and tall. The leaves were spread out in crisp surfaces in the sunshine. The stems were thicker than his finger—all from the tiny mustard seed!

The Word of God had grown too—in the heart of Jawab, in the hearts of the old chief and his wife, perhaps even in Pakoo's heart. And what about himself?

The boy stood smoothing the leaves of the luxuriant plants. They were good to eat. Should he take some home for eating? No one would see them here. Yet it seemed a desecration to break them off. Jawab must see! He must show his father! With great care he dug up two of the plants and wrapped the roots in wet leaves. He set them in his *bohongan*. They stuck out the top, so quickly had the grains of mustard grown into large plants.

There were cucumbers and squashes among the weeds, but Saksee could not bear to put anything else in the *bohongan*. The mustard plants must not be bruised or crushed.

He went to look at the tree where he had slid through the

poison caterpillars. It seemed long ago. So much had happened since then. God had saved his life.

God—who is God? The question rang again in his mind. Now he was willing to answer, "God is my Father. He loves me and I trust Him."

The grain of mustard seed was filling his heart. He walked back to the spot where the tall plants grew. It was only a short distance. There he knelt among them with his hands and his heart uplifted to the God of heaven, and there he prayed aloud for the first time.

When he returned to the village he went first to the chief's new house. Jawab was sitting in the open door, exercising his lame leg by swinging it back and forth as Rajin had taught him.

"The grain of mustard seed has grown," Saksee said, putting down the *bohongan*. He carefully lifted one of the plants and placed it in Jawab's hands.

"You mean this came from those tiny orange-colored seeds Sobat brought here?"

"Yes. Rajin gave him the seeds. We planted some in our garden and now they look like this." Saksee laid his hand on the plant. "Do you see why God's word is like a grain of mustard seed?"

The plants were perfect. They had not even wilted, because Saksee had wrapped the roots in wet leaves.

"It is beautiful!" the chief's son exclaimed, running his fingers tenderly over the fresh green leaves. Then he looked into Saksee's eyes. "What has happened to you, my friend? Your face is shining."

"Today, among the mustard plants, I prayed to God. I trust Him fully now. The love of my heart has gone out to Him."

"Then you will be baptized with me?"

"If Rajin thinks best, I will be baptized with you and Uncle Sobat and Aunt Gar and the others." Then Saksee lifted the *bohongan* and went to carry the other plant to his father.

It was now but a few days till the rest day when the baptism would take place. Excitement in both villages was great. There had never been such a thing in these mountains before. Most of all, the people talked of the messenger who came from God and promised Sobat that on the day of his baptism little Vee-Vee would hear and speak.

On the morning before the great day Rajin and Uncle Sobat came up the mountain.

"We have come to take Jawab down to Singing Water," the teacher said. "He will sleep in my house. And you, Saksee, may come along with us."

"You will stay with me," Uncle Sobat said to his nephew.

The people of Broken Light crowded around the little group as they started down the mountain.

"We will all come tomorrow," they told the four travelers. "We will come to see what the God of heaven will do."

It was a difficult thing to bring Jawab down the steep path. He was able to walk a little in some of the level spots, but there was not much level ground on the trail. Climbing down the rugged rocks was too hard for him, and at last the two men took turns carrying him on their backs. When they reached Singing Water it was afternoon and they were very tired.

When Saksee went to the pool to bathe he found many of the village people there. They were all filled with quiet gladness. From their talk he understood that they all expected something wonderful to take place tomorrow.

When evening came everyone gathered in Rajin's house

and sang the hymns with voices so sweet and tender that Saksee was glad for the falling night and the darkness of the corner where he sat, for tears of joy wet his eyes and rolled down his cheeks.

Then Rajin taught them from the Book of God. Last of all, he separated those who were to be baptized and asked them to stay when the others returned to their homes. He wanted to talk to them.

Saksee joined the group that remained. Rajin looked at him.

"Do you wish to be baptized?" the teacher asked him with a level gaze.

"Try my heart and see if I am ready," the boy said, returning the teacher's look with steady courage.

There were seventeen people besides him. He knew there would be two more tomorrow—the chief of Broken Light and his wife. Rajin asked them many questions about the teachings of God's Book. He asked them about their homes and their behavior there. Did they get angry and quarrel, or gossip or speak harshly to their loved ones? He asked about prayer. Did they know how to talk with God? Did they believe in God's Son, Jesus, who died to save them?

When the teacher had finished with the group he dismissed them, but he took hold of Saksee's arm and held him back. When the others had all gone (except Jawab who was spending the night there), he motioned the boy to sit down on the mat beside him.

"Now, tell me," he began. "I didn't know until tonight that you wish to be baptized tomorrow with the others. Why do you want to? Is this a sudden decision?"

Then Saksee told Rajin how he had hated the new teaching,

how he had fought against the God of heaven and left the village of Singing Water in order that he might never hear of God again. He told of his experience on the way up the mountain to Broken Light, when in answer to his thought of God help came. He told of his friendship with Kooning; of the deadly secret the witch doctor had entrusted to him and how he had kept that secret until it was forced from him in agony the night he lay near death from the poison caterpillars. He told how Uncle Sobat brought the grains of mustard seed. Then he told how yesterday he knelt among those green witnesses for God and prayed aloud.

"So you see," he ended the long story, "the grain of mustard seed was planted in my heart, and now it has grown and filled me. I belong to God. I talk to Him and He talks to me."

The eyes of Rajin were wet as he took the boy's hand. "You are prepared," he said. "God Himself has prepared you. You may go down with the others into the pool tomorrow."

CHAPTER 12

Vee-Vee

THE family in Uncle Sobat's house slept little that night. Every heart overflowed with solemn joy. They could not sleep for gladness. They rejoiced with one another, and the presence of God was so real in the little room that Uncle Sobat spoke to Him as to a dear friend. He thanked God for the two visits of the angel and for the promise that would come true tomorrow.

Only Vee-Vee slept. She could not hear them talking. The loudest tones did not disturb her. Uncle Sobat sat near her mat, looking often with tender gaze at this most precious child—the daughter of promise, the object of an angel's visit.

The morning of the holy rest day came at last, with long fingers of light reaching down the rugged mountainside and purple shadows shifting among the giant trees of the old forest.

Scarcely had the first glow of dawn enfolded the little hut when Rajin called at the door. He had come to gather the family for prayer.

"This is your day of blessing," he said. "It is right that we should offer special praise and thanksgiving to God this morning, and we must ask Him to make what is to happen today a glory to His name and a witness to all the people."

"This blessing will show all the people how much God loves them, even the little children," Uncle Sobat said.

Before the reverent prayer was ended the whole village stirred with life. By the time the sun rose high enough to look down on the shining pool, people began to stream down the mountain from Broken Light. They came in families and by two's and three's. A timidness was on them, as though they entered the unknown presence of a great Rajah. Their usually noisy tongues were stilled. Everyone in the village came, leaving only the family dogs behind to guard the houses. Kooning was not among them. No one knew where he had gone.

With their voices raised in rapturous song the people of Singing Water gathered at the teacher's house. With them came all the visitors from Broken Light. They crowded into the big room, filling it to overflowing, so there was no more place to sit.

All along the walls men were standing close together. Saksee stood with them. Every eye was fixed on the teacher as he explained to them the meaning of the baptism they were about to witness.

Close to the front of the room Uncle Sobat and Aunt Gar sat crowded in with the others. Vee-Vee was between her father and mother. She looked about with her usual questioning smile. Could she sense the interest of that large company of people? Could she feel the eager looks directed at her? She gave no sign. It was plain to every person gathered there that she could neither hear nor speak. Her little world of silence lay close about her, unbroken yet by any human word or earthly sound.

The service was short because there were so many visitors and the place was crowded. When it had ended the sun was approaching the zenith. The people hurried from Rajin's house down to the grassy slope by the pool. They settled themselves on rocks and stones along the margin of the water.

Aunt Gar led Vee-Vee to the water's edge and there she gave her into the care of Pakoo, who accepted the charge willingly. He held the little girl by the hand and chose a position where the child could watch the baptism with unobstructed view.

An air of expectancy filled the place. It was a solemn time. The ones who were to be baptized lined up in a double row. They waited for Rajin. He came now, walking slowly down the hill from his house, dressed in white garments. He entered the pool and led the people in another hymn. It was an old familiar song—"I Will Follow Thee, My Saviour." It was sung in the Dusun language. They all understood it.

When the singing was finished the teacher read a few words from the Word of God. Then he handed the Book to one of the men who stood near him on the shore. He went out into deeper water—deep enough for the solemn rite to be performed.

The first candidates entered the water, and the voice of song bore them along till they reached the teacher's side, one on the right hand and one on the left. He baptized them then, laying them under the water for just an instant, one after the other.

Jawab and Saksee stood next to the end of the line. Behind them—last of all—were Uncle Sobat and Aunt Gar.

Saksee felt his heart lifted into a region of peace and gladness that must be like the heaven of glory that Rajin taught them about. He looked at Jawab. His face was lighted with joy. When their turn came, Jawab walked boldly into the water. Rajin took Jawab first.

When the waters of the shining pool closed over his own head and he felt himself being lifted again, the boy knew that this was a beginning—a new birth, a new life springing up in glad and growing strength to serve and love God.

The chief's son did not lean on Saksee when they walked out of the water; he walked with a new sureness. They went straight to the spot where Pakoo still stood holding Vee-Vee by the hand.

Then, as they turned, the solemn words rang out over the stillness of the Sabbath noontime:

"I now baptize you in the name of the Father, and of the Son, and of the Holy Spirit. Amen."

Aunt Gar was taken. Then, last of all the twenty, Uncle Sobat stood ready to be buried beneath the clear water. Those who looked on his face marveled at the joy that could be seen in him. He seemed filled with ecstasy—vibrant with something that could be seen and felt. All the waiting, watching, listening multitude knew that it was joy—joy—joy, the most holy delight a man can ever know.

The only sound that broke the stillness of the moment was the gentle splash as Uncle Sobat was placed beneath the water. When he was lifted from that symbolic burial a breath like a gasp of wonder stirred the throng along the water's edge. Now every eye was fixed on Vee-Vee.

The child stood still with her hand in her Uncle Pakoo's. But now she looked eagerly toward her parents with a new alertness. They were coming toward the shore. As her father's feet touched the sand, she broke away from Pakoo and ran to meet him with outstretched arms, crying, "Father! Father!"

Her voice was clear and strong enough for all the people to hear. Uncle Sobat caught her in his arms and wept aloud in his great happiness. Fear and amazement filled every heart. Rajin stood beside them, his hands raised in blessing.

Then Vee-Vee began talking to her parents in a sweet childish voice. Her words were plain and well spoken, like any other child of six years; yet she had never heard words in all her life. The wondering people pressed closer, and seeing the many strange faces, she became suddenly shy and hid her face in the curve of her father's neck.

There was no closing hymn. The music of heaven vibrated through the company of reverent people. Speaking in hushed whispers, they started up the mountain.

It was then that Saksee saw Kooning. He was on the opposite side of the pool. He was making his way down the trunk of a branching tree. He must have hidden there early that morning. He must have watched the baptism and the wonderful miracle from his hiding place. Safely on the ground, he gathered his garments about him and disappeared into the jungle.

Saksee and Pakoo returned with the other villagers to Broken Light. Jawab needed no help on the return journey. Some said it was because his great joy gave him new strength; but Jawab walked without difficulty from that day.

Nothing was ever the same again in the village of Broken Light. The people were so eager to hear more of the God-teaching that several of the families decided to move down the mountain. They built their huts close to the others in Singing Water.

A church was built, and also a school, where Jawab and Saksee and the other young people of both villages went every day to learn reading and writing and the teachings of God's Book, and how to make many useful things with their hands.

The youngest pupil in the school was Vee-Vee. She learned fast, and Uncle Sobat's greatest pleasure was to sit on his mat in the evening and listen to his little daughter read from the Book of God.

Pakoo came down the mountain and settled in Singing Water. When the next baptism day came, he was ready to show his trust in God by following his son in that sacred rite.

Then, after many days, Rajin sat one evening in the large room of his house where the village people used to gather for worship before the fine new church was built. He looked out over the valley. Saksee was with him, and Jawab too. The three of them were working together now. The two younger ones were training to become teachers themselves. Just as the sun threw its last lingering rays across the lovely mountain scene they all saw a lone figure coming toward the house.

"It is Kooning!" Jawab exclaimed in wonder.

"Why would he come here?" Saksee asked.

Rajin went to meet him, and he helped the old man to a comfortable place on the mat beside them.

"It is no use," the witch doctor said. "I cannot get away from God. He follows me everywhere. I hear His voice and I am covered with shame and sorrow that I have fought against Him. I have tried to do terrible things to those who followed Him."

The old man's voice broke with grief. "Tell me, is there any hope for such a murderer—such a wicked man as I?"

Then they all comforted him with words of kindness and affection. Rajin promised to teach him the new good magic from the Word of God. The boys agreed to help him learn to read. It was hard to tell whose joy was greatest, for none of them had been so happy since the day Vee-Vee became like other children.

When they left the teacher's house they walked together, Kooning in the middle and Jawab and Saksee on either side.

"You know," Saksee said as they came to Uncle Sobat's house, "we must tell him the good news first."

"What is the good news?" Kooning asked in wonder.

"That God can save any of us—any of us, at any time," Jawab answered.

Then Saksee turned and took one of Kooning's hands and one of Jawab's in his own. "One of the best parts of the good news is this—you cannot run away from God."